A Child's Delight

❧

NOEL PERRIN

Dartmouth College

Published by University Press of New England

Hanover and London

for Alexandra Hess

who, though less than two years old,

is in some ways the cause of this book

Dartmouth College
Published by University Press of New England,
37 Lafayette St., Lebanon, NH 03766
This collection © 1997 by the Trustees of Dartmouth College
First Dartmouth/University Press of New England paperback edition 2003
Printed in the United States of America   5 4 3 2 1
CIP data appear at the end of the book

The essays on Lucy Boston, Robert Burch, Lolah Burford, Edward Eager, Rumer Godden, Virginia Hamilton, Nathaniel Hawthorne, Jean Merrill, Mary Norton, Earnest Seton, Dodie Smith, Zilpha Snyder, Mary Stolz, and T. H. White appeared first in the Washington *Post,* usually under different titles and in somewhat different form. © 1990, 1991, 1992, The Washington Post. Reprinted with permission. The essays on Anne Lindbergh and Noel Streatfeild first appeared in the Los Angeles *Times,* also in slightly different form. The author is grateful to both for permission to reprint.

CONTENTS

Contents   vii

PREFACE

Unlike adults, children have no easy access to literary guides. What they read is usually random. If lucky, they'll be given a few of the classics of children's literature as birthday and Christmas presents. They may bump up against a few others in school. A handful they may see transformed into videos.

But there are many wonderful minor classics and even some major ones they are apt to miss altogether—unless a parent or an uncle or a godmother steps in. This book is designed to assist steppers-in. It consists of thirty short essays, each about a wonderful but little-known book for children. Little-known to children, I mean, and also to most parents, godparents, etc. Some are very well known to children's book editors and librarians, and to people who work in the children's sections of good bookstores.

This brings up a key question. How do I know which of the classics *are* little known to readers, and which are so familiar that they need no recommending? Well, I can best answer with a story. It's a story that begins at a considerable remove from the question. But have faith. It does get there.

Back in the 1980s I wrote a monthly column for the Sunday book section of the Washington *Post*. It was called "Rediscoveries." Each of these monthly essays focused on a neglected minor masterpiece for grown-ups, with the avowed purpose of luring people into reading it. In 1988 I collected most of these essays in a book called *A Reader's Delight,* to which you are holding the sequel.

In due course that column ended, because I had used up my entire lifetime collection of neglected minor masterpieces. Several years passed. Then the *Post* invited me to resume. Only now the column would be called "Rediscoveries for Children," and would draw on an entirely different set of books. Having had first two children of my own and later four stepchildren to read to, and having read aloud for two or three thousand nights so far; having had a mother who wrote books for children, and later a wife who wrote even better books for children; having of course once been a child myself, and one addicted to reading, I have had virtually a whole lifetime in which to learn about marvelous books written for the young. I felt ready.

The day the *Post* formally invited me, I was in Washington. My wife had a new book out, and she had come down from Vermont for a signing and a reading. I had come with her because we like to stay together. But I also had a little business to do.

While Anne was charming the socks off a bunch of ten year olds, I was having lunch with an editor at the *Post*, and he was telling me to go ahead with the new column. But not quite with carte blanche. "Before you start writing," he said, "why don't you send me a list of, oh, say the first eight or ten books you propose to include?"

It was a stifling hot day in Washington, and I had no great wish to leave the cool restaurant where we had just finished an excellent meal. "Never mind sending. I'll give you the list right now," I said, and pulled out the notebook I generally keep in my pocket. On the first clean page I wrote, T. H. White, *Mistress Masham's Repose.*

The editor nodded approvingly. "Good choice. That book is famous among librarians, but most kids and most parents have never heard of it. Yes. Let's start with that. What's your next?"

I wrote, Dodie Smith, *I Capture the Castle,* and he gave me a pat on the shoulder, he was so pleased. "I thought I was the only person in Washington who knew that book," he said.

"Well, there used to be two of you," I answered. "My

wife used to live in Washington, and she's the person who introduced me to Dodie Smith."

He smiled. "Send her back. We need her. What's number three?"

And here the trouble began. Without hesitation I wrote, Margery Sharp, *The Rescuers*.

He shook his head. "No. I don't think you can use that. Far too well known. There's even a movie."

"No problem," I said cheerfully. "I've got tons more." And I wrote, E. Nesbit, *The Phoenix and the Carpet*.

"E. Nesbit? You really think she's obscure enough? I don't. Anyway, we ran a piece about her just a couple of years ago. Won't work."

So it went. In the end I wrote down the titles of seventeen books. He accepted nine and rejected eight. The problem was never that he didn't think a book good enough; it was always that he considered it too famous, too obvious, too predictable a choice. Why run a piece recommending a book everyone knows already?

That night, on the train going home to Vermont, I naturally told my wife about the lunch and the list. "Do you really think Nesbit is that famous?" I asked.

"Why don't you find out?" she said. "You've got a lot of students. Ask them."

I *do* have a lot of students. I teach American literature at Dartmouth College. That very term I had a course with fifty-four students enrolled.

Two days later I gave them an extra quiz, one for which they needed to prepare not at all. The quiz simply listed nineteen authors in alphabetical order, and named one book for each author. These were the seventeen books the editor and I had talked about, plus a tiny control group. This consisted of *The Hobbit* and *Charlotte's Web*. The Washington editor and I might differ about the degree of fame possessed by Nesbit or Sharp, but we could hardly argue about J. R. R. Tolkien and E. B. White. Here were the absolutely famous. Let's see how much lesser the others were.

The format of the quiz was simple. By each of the nineteen titles I drew two little boxes. If a student had heard of the book, he or she checked the first box. If they had actually read it, they also checked the second. The whole quiz took about a minute.

Four students had cut class that day, so I got a nice, round, statistically impressive fifty answers. These answers so surprised me that I decided to check them, and make sure Dartmouth students aren't a bibliological anomaly. (They aren't.) The next week I got a friend who teaches at Exeter to give the quiz to fifty of his high school-age students. With a few minor variations, the results were the same. I thus wound up with numbers for one hundred exceptionally well-educated and presumably well-read Americans. They're so interesting that I'm going to print the whole list right here. (See table 1.)

The editor, you will recall, had said no to eight of these books. I have to admit that with two exceptions he had unerringly rejected the best known. He had said not to do *The Story of Ferdinand,* for example, and was he ever right! More than half the students had heard of it, and a full third had read it, or had had it read to them. On Nesbit and Horwood, however, he was mistaken. If only two people out of a hundred have read a book, and if those hundred are part of the prime reading group in the whole country, you really cannot say the book is well known.

But the most interesting thing about the survey, I think, is that except for *Ferdinand* and the two control books, you can't call *any* of these books well known. Yes, 12 percent of these bright students had read *A Wizard of Earthsea,* and over a fifth had heard of it. But think of the four-fifths who hadn't; think of the 88 percent who had never read so much as the marvelous opening sentence. Isn't it fair to write for

Table 1

The original 17 books	Heard of it	Actually read it
Lloyd Alexander, *The Book of Three*	37	20
Lucy Boston, *The Children of Green Knowe*	11	3
Robert Burch, *Queenie Peavey*	10	2
Edward Eager, *Half Magic*	12	7
Rumer Godden, *The Dolls' House*	29*	5
Virginia Hamilton, *The Planet of Junior Brown*	8	0
Nathaniel Hawthorne, *Tanglewood Tales*	20	3
William Horwood, *Duncton Wood*	6	2
Monroe Leaf, *The Story of Ferdinand*	52	34
Ursula Le Guin, *A Wizard of Earthsea*	22	12
Jean Merrill, *The Pushcart War*	42	18
E. Nesbit, *The Phoenix and the Carpet*	2	2
Margery Sharp, *The Rescuers*	22	15
Dodie Smith, *I Capture the Castle*	1	0
Zilpha Keatley Snyder, *The Egypt Game*	8	1
Mary Stolz, *A Dog on Barkham Street*	12	9
T. H. White, *Mistress Masham's Repose*	3	2

The control group	Heard of it	Actually read it
J. R. R. Tolkien, *The Hobbit*	91	62
E. B. White, *Charlotte's Web*	94	90

*I don't entirely trust this figure. It may be Ibsen's play that some of them had heard of.

them? I think it is. And if it's fair for Le Guin, it's fair for nearly all the others.

So with some regret I dropped *Ferdinand,* which was my favorite book when I was four, and which still melts me when I look at Robert Lawson's drawing of the corks growing on a Spanish cork tree, or at the expression in the eye of the bee that Ferdinand is about to sit on. I would have loved to write an essay about the book.

But all the others I have felt free to write about——if not in the *Post,* then elsewhere. Two of the sixteen survivors I did wind up dropping, but that was because when I reread them, I found them, though still good, less so than I had remembered.

Looking beyond the list from the cool restaurant, looking at the whole range of children's literature, I have obviously picked books that I admire and that my children and stepchildren loved. I have also followed a simple rule. I checked each group of books with a group of students. If more than 10 or 20 percent had read it, it did not get in. The Narnia books, for example, didn't have a prayer, nor did *Little Women,* the *Little House* books, Kipling's *Jungle Book, Winnie-the-Pooh,* or Nancy Drew. (She, I admit, I never considered including. I was just curious about her popularity. It is real. It is also considerably less than Tolkien's or White's.)

There is just one more thing to be said. In no sense does this book systematically cover children's literature. It's a bouquet, not a botany text. It is tilted toward the twentieth century, partly because this century really has been the golden age of children's literature, but partly because I feel uneasy with the insistent moralizing of many of the earlier classics, like Charles Kingsley's *Water Babies* and John Ruskin's *The King of the Golden River.* (I don't like the quite different moralizing tone of some modern stuff, either, and you will find none of that in here.)

But now it's time to turn to the actual books.

Thetford Center, Vermont   N.P.

◈ 1 ◈

A Good Book to Read to
a Two Year Old

EATRIX POTTER was not the only person, a hundred years ago, who spent her days writing soon-
to-be-classic picture books for small children.
There was also Leslie Brooke. Ms. Potter wrote and illustrated her best-known book, *The Tale of Peter Rabbit*, in
1902. Mr. Brooke wrote and illustrated *Johnny Crow's Garden* in 1903.

It's not a book I recommend because of its plot. There *is*
a story, to be sure, but it's not the kind that keeps either you
or a two year old on the edge of your seat. It goes like this.
Somewhere in England lives a crow who loves to garden.
Despite his being a bird of good family, clearly a gentleman
(you can tell by the pictures), he personally does all the
work. As Brooke succinctly puts it:

> Johnny Crow
> Would dig and sow
> Till he made a little Garden.

English understatement. That garden is not little, it's
huge. (You can tell by the pictures.) It even has ornamental
topiary, including an arched entranceway with the word
"Welcome" spelled out in living green.

A real garden by real crows, I think, would consist entirely of corn. If they did put in a few other things, they would stick entirely to the faster growing and more nutritious vegetables.

Johnny, however, hasn't so much as a row of radishes. His is a vast flower garden. What you see him doing in the first picture is planting sweet peas; the beautifully drawn spade with which he prepared their bed lies nearby. In the second he is standing on one foot, watering pansies with the kind of handsome metal watering can they used in pre-plastic 1903.

But back to the story. Johnny has his garden ready in just two pictures and sixteen words. Now what? Now other animals, entering under the Welcome sign, flock in for a garden party. Some are what they fondly believe to be well-dressed:

> And the Lion
> Had a green and yellow tie on
> In Johnny Crow's Garden.

In actual fact, the tie is far too big, even for a lion of such size. Furthermore, its pale green and yellow clash horribly with his tawny mane. But the lion strides about looking extremely pleased with himself. And Johnny, out of pure kindly good feeling, paces along with him, having first donned a small and elegant red tie that goes very well with his dark feathers. None of this, of course, is expressed in the lion-section text, which consists solely of the three lines quoted above.

Next to arrive is a rat, wearing a princely feather in his hat, who strolls by the pansies. What makes him the dashing figure he is, though, is not so much the feather as the way he has looped his tail under his left arm so that it repeats the curve of his feather on a still grander scale. He looks both cavalier and meditative. Johnny is not in sight here; the rat needs nothing.

Now comes a bear, wearing no clothes at all. He feels embarrassed. In the background, the lion sits on a garden bench, looking smug. Still further back some small animals appear to be playing cricket. Johnny is right there, looking concerned. And in a matter of four wonderful illustrations and thirteen words of text, he has arranged with two apes —a tailor and his assistant—to make the bear a frock coat and striped trousers. In the fourth of these pictures the clothes are made; the bear is wearing them; he looks terrific and he knows it. Snout lifted high, he is just parading past the lion, whose oversize tie is now drooping a bit and who has a distinctly worried expression. Johnny is nowhere to be seen. The bear problem being solved, he is off doing nice things for other guests.

By no means the whole book is concerned with apparel. Many of the things that can happen at an outdoor party, such as bad weather, do happen, plus several things that are not normally part of social entertaining. Here's the full text of the weather incident:

> Then the Crane
> Was caught in the Rain
> In Johnny Crow's Garden.

The words are nothing—or, rather, nothing but rhyme and a certain incantatory quality to the refrain that is quite separate from meaning. But the three pictures! In the first, the Crane has drawn itself up as tall and slender as it can, next to the trunk of a sapling tree. Obviously this is so as to present minimal area to the rain. In the second, J. Crow has arrived and is proffering an umbrella on his outstretched wings, while the Crane bends gratefully down to take it. In the third, the Crane is speeding down a wet garden path with umbrella open, while Johnny sprints along behind, probably getting soaked.

Then there is the Stork, giving a Philosophic Talk to a

somewhat mutinous audience, the Whale telling a story so long and dull that *his* audience gradually dwindles to just Johnny, and finally the Fox locks all the guests into the kind of open-air pillory known as a stocks. The Giraffe, with his legs splayed out and his neck fastened down at almost ground level, looks especially uncomfortable.

> But Johnny Crow
> He let them go
> And they all sat down
> to their dinner in a row.

You can be sure that Johnny will feed them well.

For a two year old, the delight is in the many absurdities in the pictures and in the funny rhymes in the text. For the adult reading the book aloud, there is another level of pleasure. For example, the learned Stork gets more and more philosophic:

> Till the Hippopotami
> Said "Ask no further 'What am I?'"

As a small boy, hearing the book read to me by my mother, I had no idea that "hippopotami" was the proper Greek plural for hippopotamus, nor would I have much cared if I had known. I just loved the triple rhyme. But as an adult reading to my own children, I am tickled by the propriety, not to mention the incipient identity crisis, in what the Stork is saying. And I am even more tickled by the titles of the books that professorial bird has brought along.

If you look hard (and know how to read), you will see that one of the books is by Confucius, only here it's spelled Confuseous. Another of the Stork's books has both title and author in Latin. Well, sort of. Ludovicus Carrollus, *De Jabberwockibus* appears on the cover. It was thirty-two years since Lewis Carroll had published *Through the Looking-Glass* with its contained poem "Jabberwocky," and here was Leslie Brooke paying discreet tribute to a literary ancestor. And equally, making discreet admission that hippopotami and what-am-I will signify no more to very small children than the nonsense words of "Jabberwocky" do to adults. Only . . . they will later.

Am I reading this in, attributing to Leslie Brooke a thought he never had? I am not. Many years later Brooke explicitly commented on things the two year old will miss: "The child does not mind a bit if there are things he does not quite understand." To which I add: It's important that there *be* things he or she doesn't understand, or understands only partly, by guessing from the context. That's an excellent way to learn.

Books for very young children don't have to be Dick and Janeish, or even *Goodnight Moon*ish. I see no need to dumb down in writing for the young. Why not smarten up instead? Brooke did.

Johnny Crow's Garden.
Leslie Brooke. 1903.

❧ 2 ❧

Wanda's Wonder-Book

ONCE THERE was a little girl named Wanda. She was the eldest child of an artist named Anton Gág and his wife Lissi. Along with her five younger sisters and her one brother, Wanda grew up in a small town in Minnesota.

All seven of the children were artistically gifted, and all "began to draw as soon as they could hold a pencil." (I'm quoting Rebecca Keim in a book called *Three Women Artists*.)

But the children didn't just draw. They also made music, told stories, decorated eggs, loved to write. Let's look in on a typical evening, say in the year 1905. Wanda is twelve. The whole family is gathered in the living room, which is unlike any other living room in New Ulm, Minnesota—and unlike 99.99 percent of living rooms in the United States. Among his many artistic activities, Anton paints murals, and he has completely covered the ceiling with cherubs and clouds.

Down below, on the mortal earth (or, more precisely, on the floor of the living room), the whole family is grouped around the piano. Lissi plays, and they all sing. Another evening it might be perfectly quiet in the house, because everyone except the baby is busy drawing. A third evening, one of the children might be reading a story aloud, usually one she had written herself. Poor kids, what else could they do with their evenings? They grew up not only pre-television but pre-radio.

Though Anton and Lissi probably wouldn't have had a TV set anyway. Being Bohemians, they would have scorned to. Anton in fact was a double bohemian. Bohemian with a capital B because he grew up in that part of the Austro-Hungarian empire called Bohemia, where his father had been a wood-carver. He only came to the United States in 1873. Bohemian with a small b, as was Lissi, because he was unconventional, non-bourgeois, what was then called a free spirit. I'm not just thinking of the cherub-covered ceiling and the row of little girls busy making sketches. Anton was determined to make his living from art, whether that was a practical idea or not, and in New Ulm, Minnesota, at the turn of the century, it was a resoundingly impractical one. As Rebecca Keim temperately puts it, Anton was "an exceptionally competent easel painter in an area where the market for such work was limited." That's your true bohemian: a starving artist.

But it's one thing to starve alone in a garret, and quite another to have seven hungry little faces looking at you down the table. So Anton found a new art. The average American at the turn of the century may not have cared greatly about easel painting or cherubs, but he would buy a photograph, so Anton and Lissi opened a photographer's studio, and they scraped by. Later Anton even got an occasional commission for a mural in a courthouse or a church.

But bohemians, lower-case, are often physically frail; artists often die young. When Wanda was fourteen, her father fell ill, and when she was fifteen he died. The last words he spoke were to her, whom he considered the most talented of all his children. She must be the successful artist, he told her, that he himself had never quite managed to be.

Wanda was in ninth grade when her father died. She had a few things to do before she could become a major artist, like finish high school and help her grieving mother raise the younger children. They had almost no money. Anton's year-long illness had been costly, and health insurance was far in the future, like TV.

Wanda helped a lot—was even a second mother—and her financial contribution came entirely through art. As a high school student, she designed and sold greeting cards. She gave drawing lessons. Best of all, she began to sell both drawings and stories to the children's section of a Minneapolis newspaper. (Poor Minneapolis kids: no TV.) In one two-year period she sold thirty-five pictures, fourteen stories (ten of which she also illustrated), and four poems.

After graduation she briefly lapsed into prudence, and spent one non-artistic year teaching school. She was nineteen. Then she got scholarships: first to an art school in St. Paul and eventually to the Art Students League in New York. She never finished the course. Soon after she got to New York, her mother died, which left it to her to finish raising the younger children. She dropped out of the League, moved those children still at home to New York, and supported them all by doing commercial art. In the variety of artistic schemes to make money that she thought of, she showed herself to be her father's true daughter. She painted lamp shades. She did fashion illustrations. She designed interesting toys. And—my favorite—in 1925 she began syndicating a series of picture puzzles that she called Wanda's Wonderland. She was now thirty-two. She had raised the children, she was enjoying a bohemian life in New York City, she had become financially successful. But she had done no major work yet, nothing to fulfill a deathbed promise.

Then, three years later, the miracle occurred. Wanda published her first book, a picture book for small children. It's called *Millions of Cats,* and it has stayed in print from that moment to this.

It is a very simple book with a very simple story. An old

man and an old woman live in a "nice clean house which had flowers all around it, except where the door was." What perfect phrasing those last five words are—exactly how a child would see it or say it.

But the old couple are lonesome. "'If only we had a cat,' sighed the very old woman." So the old man sets off to find her one.

What he finds is like the Gág family, only more so. In the famous refrain that runs through the book, he comes on a hill and sees:

Cats here, cats there,
Cats and kittens everywhere,
Hundreds of cats,
Thousands of cats,
Millions and billions and trillions of cats.

He selects one cat to take home. But then he sees another so appealing that he picks that one, too. Then a third, a fourth, and finally he picks the whole several trillion. They all accompany him, and they are like a force of nature. They come to a pond, they all take a drink—and the pond is dry. Now they are hungry. Each cat eats one bite of grass (this is not sound natural history, like *Watership Down*), and the hills are bare.

The old woman is much startled when the procession arrives: "'My dear!' she cried, 'What are you doing? I asked for one little cat, and what do I see?—'" Then she speaks the refrain. After that she adds, "We can never feed them all."

The ending of the book is actually quite bloody. The old woman asks the cats (they are talking cats) to select the prettiest one of all, for her to keep. The ensuing brawl is so violent that she and the old man run into the house (which may possibly have cherubs on the ceiling) to avoid the noise. Both of them are gentle and peace-loving.

When it's finally quiet again, and they come out, only

one kitten is left; the rest have performed the anatomical impossibility of all eating each other. The old couple is happy with the one kitten left.

The ending doesn't *feel* bloody, though, and that's because it's obvious to a child from the very first wonderful drawing that these are not flesh-and-blood cats, or people, either. Everything is stylized, symmetrical, incantatory—and almost perfectly timeless. *Millions of Cats* is one of those rare books that feels on publication day as if it had been part of our literature for a couple of centuries. It was seen as an instant classic in 1928, and it remains as pure a delight today as it was then. To those who know the history of the author's family, there is a little extra pleasure in being aware that there is one touch of collaboration. Wanda wrote all the words, and drew all the pictures. But she didn't do the very pretty hand lettering in which the story is told. That's the work of another of the seven talented Gágs, her younger brother Joseph.

One doesn't repeat a success as nearly perfect as this one. Though like both parents she died early, Wanda had time to produce half a dozen other books. All are worth looking at for their art, and the one called *Nothing at All* is also worth reading for the story, provided you and the child you are reading to have a tolerance for a slightly mechanical plot structure. But only *Millions of Cats* is up there in the empyrean, safe among the cherubs and clouds. Anton would have been proud.

Millions of Cats.
Wanda Gág. 1928.

❧ 3 ❧

The Third Grade Goes to Space

*H*ERE'S A preposterous situation. An ordinary school bus, on its way to a planetarium, suddenly develops rocket drive and heads straight for the moon. The passengers, a class of third graders, find they are wearing space suits, and they pile out at once onto the surface of the moon. Their red-haired teacher, who has been first driving and then flying the bus, hurries off with them. *Her* space suit is bright pink and slightly magical. That is, it's covered with the stars and moons and comets that give authority to an astrologer's robe. She has some of that authority. Her name is Ms. Frizzle.

When she has the class calmed down a bit, Ms. Frizzle gives a brief lesson in lunology. Maybe three sentences worth. Much more moon data, however, appears less directly. For example: A scale, the kind that tells your fortune as well as your weight, conveniently materializes near a crater. A plump third grader named Arnold steps on, and finds he now weighs fourteen pounds instead of his customary eighty-five. The scale prints out a card that reads, "You will travel to far-off places." Since he is *in* a far-off place, this seems a safe prediction. Not to mention one that will amuse third graders. It's their kind of irony.

Another example: Two very short themes by members of the class (one is only sixteen words long), handwritten on lined paper, appear to the right of what is otherwise a two-page spread showing Arnold on the scale, Ms. Frizzle giving her one-minute class, and two girls who have thoughtfully brought a jump rope swinging it while a third girl and a boy jump spectacularly high. All wearing their space helmets, of course.

A plot is also thickening. An insufferable little girl named Janet is watching the jumpers. She is Arnold's cousin, just visiting his school for the day, and she has already turned off nearly everyone in the third grade by her boastfulness. Typical Janet remarks: "Our swings are better than your swings." "We have *new* school buses at our school." "I have five computers."

Looking now at the moon-leapers, Janet speaks again. "I was in a national jump-rope contest," she informs the group. "I won, of course."

"Just ignore her," a boy in blue space boots advises.

Ms. Frizzle soon herds everybody back on the bus, and they head straight for the sun (where they most assuredly do not land). She gives another tiny lecture. Janet gets in a few more boasts. The bus then works its way out through the solar system, landing on every planet, all of them conveniently equipped with scales and all of the scales patronized by Arnold. When they reach the asteroid belt, though, something bad happens. A fragment of interstellar rock smashes into one of the bus's taillights, and Ms. Frizzle unwisely goes out to check the damage, leaving the bus on autopilot.

While she is out there, the autopilot malfunctions. Her tether line picks that moment to snap, and the bus heads on out to Jupiter with no adult aboard. And now boastful Janet saves the day. Only she has the presence of mind to search the bus's glove compartment, where she finds both Ms. Frizzle's lesson plan (Janet takes over as teacher for the outer planets), and also the manual for the autopilot. Everyone, including Ms. Frizzle, gets safely back to earth, and no one's family believes them when they tell about their day. There had been a trip scheduled, all right, but it was only to the planetarium, not to space.

This is a bare-bones account of an irresistible book called *The Magic School Bus, Lost in the Solar System.* The words, written by Joanna Cole, are every one of them just right. The pictures, drawn by Bruce Degen, are bright, clear, imaginative, funny when they should be funny, serious (with a few peripheral jokes) when seriousness is called for. It's called for when the third graders first see the rings of Saturn, for example.

Clearly the book is intended as a painless but scientific introduction to the solar system, and just as clearly it succeeds.

I might as well admit that when I first saw the book, I didn't expect to like it so much. There are, in the abstract, a lot of counts against it.

To begin with, like so many children's books, it is part of a series—and a series with a formula. Cole and Degen have done half a dozen Magic Bus science books, and all of them use the identical multimedia mix. That is, there is a main narrative in a nicely printed typeface, a paragraph or two of which appears on almost every page. On every page there is also much cartoon-style conversation, hand-lettered, in balloons, according to the best comic-strip conventions. (One exception: Comic strips virtually never employ periods at the ends of sentences. It's exclamation points or nothing. But Cole and Degen, civilized persons that they are, use periods quite freely.)

There is also a third element: those short, hand-lettered student papers. Any scientific information that doesn't fit comfortably into the main narrative or in the cartoon dialogue can easily be popped into these little themes. It was a clever idea, back in 1986, to use eleven of them in the first Magic Bus book. But to have twenty-seven of them in *Lost in the Solar System!* By all rights it ought to be a mere gimmick by now, a weariness to the reader. But it's not. It stays as fresh as this morning's dew, which is in no way staled by the fact that there was also dew yesterday, and the day before, etc.

In theory, I don't think much of multimedia books. Yes, I know that human beings are multimedia creatures—seeing, hearing, touching, smelling all at once, and sometimes tasting, too. The fact remains that most multimedia publishing is a lot stronger in technical cleverness than it is in merit, let alone any touch of genius. But it works with Degen and Cole.

Here's another objection. One of the standard complaints about end-of-the-twentieth-century American culture is that we reduce everything to sound bites. If you can't say it in thirty seconds, don't say it at all. And if that means that everything must be oversimplified, well, too bad. This is the TV age. A whole minute costs too much money, and besides, the audience might get bored and switch channels.

Lost in the Solar System is, of course, designed entirely in sound bites. Ms. Frizzle talks in them. So do the kids. They also write in them. The longest of the student themes runs to thirty-seven words, and the average length is closer to twenty.

But the fact is that the three media work together to produce a complex and entertaining account of the solar system, a sort of verbal orrery. Enough bites of the right kind make a meal.

One final objection. What's this magic doing in a book that is supposed to describe the solar system scientifically? Must we pander *that* much to the popular mind? Surely the science will get contaminated.

In theory and sometimes in fact I'd say yes, it will indeed. For example, it's clear to me that science fiction descends to mere space opera the minute the author begins to sneak in magic clad in scientific terms. A common piece of magic is the "space warp," which enables starships to travel faster than the speed of light. There is no scientific theory of space warps. None. They're just handy for getting short-lived human beings across the galaxy. Until a reputable theory of faster-than-light travel arises (which is doubtful), no serious science fiction writer will employ the concept. Nor any other magic, such as beaming people up.

All the same, a mixture of magic and science works just fine in *Lost in the Solar System*. Partly that's because third graders are too young and whimsical to be held to grown-up standards here. Mainly it's because Cole and Degen sneak nothing in, blur no boundaries, are instead completely open. No kid is left in doubt as to what is real science and what is playful magic. Even if somehow one were still in doubt, the last page of each book would set them straight. Here the magic is firmly but funnily denied. These denials on the last page of *Lost* are all too long to quote. (For once, no sound bites.) That's OK. My favorite example comes from an earlier book, anyway. In this book the class is investigating the weather, and the bus skips around the atmosphere as readily as scales pop up for Arnold. One of the notes on the last page reads, "Once a bus is left behind in a cloud, it *cannot* suddenly appear in the school parking lot all by itself. Obviously, someone has to go back to the cloud and drive it home."

How can you resist a disclaimer like that?

The Magic School Bus, Lost in the Solar System.
Joanna Cole and Bruce Degen. 1990.

❧ 4 ❧

Living Dolls

*I*T COMES EASILY to human beings to imagine that anything that *looks* like a living creature must *be* a living creature. Or at least must have the potential to come to life. Say it's a statue—the marble representation of a girl. The young man Pygmalion can put his arms around it, and hardly feel surprised at all when he feels hugged in return and finds a living girl smiling at him.

More scarily, say it's a portrait by a good artist, the portrait of an old man. The artist did the eyes so well that no matter where you stand the portrait seems to be looking straight at you. You almost can't help feeling that the thing is alive, and you wonder uneasily what its intentions are. At least you might if you're alone in the room with it, and it's night, and there's no one within call.

Such thoughts come most easily to children, of course, and hence much of the appeal of dolls, stuffed animals, and toy soldiers. Dolls especially hover on the edge of life. Any child knows perfectly well that at the moment it goes to sleep its dolls may wake up. Quite possibly they have been alive and conscious all the time, but now in the dark, empty room they are able to move around. That's why one careful little girl I know always shuts hers in a heavy-lidded toy chest at night. She thinks they're not strong enough to get the lid up.

Children's literature is full of stories about dolls that come to life. The English novelist Rumer Godden alone has written seven or eight books with doll characters, interspersed among her adult novels.

Hers are not scary doll stories. There is nothing to frighten a timid child, no tiny evil figures climbing up the bed posts. On the contrary, her dolls are quite harmless. Though alive and conscious, they are rarely able to move unless picked up by a child. What they want is to be loved. And held, and played with, and given things. Pretty much the same treatment children want from their parents.

Rumer Godden usually writes better for adults, I think, than she does for children. Her doll books and her mouse books tend to be easily sentimental, and some of the later ones have a far worse fault: They are written to formula. Even *Impunity Jane*—about an adventurous doll who hates being stuck in a dollhouse and longs to roam the world in a child's pocket (and after almost a hundred years of waiting, achieves that in the pocket of a small boy named Gabriel)— even that seems to me a bit too pat.

But there are two exceptions. The lesser one is *The Story of Holly and Ivy*. Anyone who knows English Christmas carols will instantly guess that this is a Christmas story. Ivy is a child and Holly is a doll, and no one wants either of them for Christmas. Except that at the last possible moment, on Christmas morning itself, each is adopted. Ivy gets a mother, and Holly gets Ivy. Sentimental? You bet. But *very* well told.

The major exception is *The Dolls' House*. This was the first doll book that Ms. Godden wrote, back in 1947, and it has the freshness of a discovery. It also has a lot more than that: It has wonderful characters and a wonderful situation. It has wonderful illustrations, too—though these, of course, are to the credit of the American illustrator, Tasha Tudor. I especially like the cover.

The main characters are a family of dolls owned by two

little girls in London. The doll parents are Mr. and Mrs. Plantagenet—he a rather fragile china doll, with brown hair and brown glass eyes, she a cheap celluloid doll that originally came in a Christmas cracker. Actually, it's only the little girls who call her Mrs. Plantagenet; the other dolls call her Birdie. She is not quite right in the head—literally. There's something inside the celluloid that rattles. But she is a loving, devoted doll-mother.

Then there are two children: a girl named Tottie and a boy named Apple. Age works differently with dolls than with people. Tottie is a wooden Dutch doll with painted hair and eyes; she first belonged to the great-grandmother of the little girls. In strict chronology, she is thus far older than Birdie, her mother, whom the little girls only got in the Christmas cracker a couple of years ago. Apple is a cloth doll, very small, and he is the baby brother. Finally, there is a toy dog named Darner.

These five live in a shoebox in a London flat, and are much played with by the two little girls. It is cold and dark in the shoebox, and what they wish, of course, is that they had a dollhouse to live in. The book is the story of how they do get one—but with it, they get one of its doll inhabitants from long ago: a beautiful and cold-hearted bridal doll named Marchpane. No threat at all to the little girls (on the contrary, they are fascinated by her, and begin to neglect their doll family for her), she is a menace indeed to the Plantagenets. For a time it looks as if they will become Marchpane's servants, and all be thrust together in the attic of the dollhouse, while Marchpane has the rest of the house to herself. At the end they are saved, but at the cost of Birdie's life.

Rumer Godden was clearly replicating two things with her doll family: the real situation in London in 1947, and the position of children at any time. No human being was living in a shoebox in London then, but the city was full of bomb sites, and many were living in horribly cramped quarters.

The well-built old dollhouse that the two little girls refurbish was a miniature of what millions of English people would have dreamed of getting. And whether consciously nor not, Ms. Godden made a statement of her hope for postwar England when she has Birdie and her family get the house instead of upper-class Marchpane, who wanted all the rooms to herself.

More interesting still is the parallel between dolls and children. With rare exceptions, the Plantagenets can't act, nor Marchpane; what they can do is feel and wish and hope. And sometimes their wishes influence people. There is a quite moving scene where Birdie wishes and wishes she could have a feather bed. Emily and Charlotte, the little girls who own her, had been about to make her one of cotton wool. Then (as she thinks) the idea just comes to Charlotte that a feather bed would be nicer. There is a clear and encouraging message to children that just because you're little and weak, it doesn't mean you can't ever influence events. These dolls influence many.

Ms. Godden does as well with the human characters as with the dolls. Emily and Charlotte's parents are shadowy background figures, and even Mrs. Innisfree, the resourceful family friend who is so helpful in getting the old dollhouse furniture refinished, is lightly sketched. But Emily and Charlotte themselves are a wonderful study. They seem to be about nine and seven. Emily is the elder who is used to having all the good ideas, and Charlotte is the affectionate, biddable younger sister, who is just beginning to have thoughts of her own. Take away the dolls, and you would still have two very appealing little girls.

The book has for me just one fault: It is a little too conscious of its readers. I take it for granted that it began as stories told aloud to Ms. Godden's own two daughters, and when she made it into a book, she kept the sort of interpolations that a parent does put in when telling a make-believe. For example, there is a moment when Emily has decided to lend Tottie, the wooden Dutch doll, to a doll exhibition. She's going to be paid a little, and she wants the money for fixing up the old dollhouse. But Tottie doesn't want to go, rightly fearing that she may never come back. Ms. Godden writes this: "Emily felt reproach and misery from Tottie, but she did not understand why. Can you guess why?" Hell, yes, I can, and I wish the question weren't there.

A very tiny fault in a very good book. In many senses, Rumer Godden brings things to life.

The Dolls' House.
Rumer Godden. 1947.

❧ 5 ❧

Boy Wants Dog

WHAT DO GROWN-UPS hope to accomplish when they give a book to a child? Well, first, obviously, they want to give the child pleasure. From this point of view, and depending on the child's tastes, Nancy Drew and *Charlotte's Web* make equally good presents.

But of course grown-ups have lots of other objectives, and parents do especially. They may hope to encourage a currently nonreading child to become more of a reader, and hence try to pick as effortless a book as possible. (Depending on the child's tastes, Nancy Drew may be ahead here.)

They may also be thinking about the child's real life. Say they have just moved from Wisconsin to Washington, depriving their son of a chance to go into fifth grade with his Milwaukee friends. He minds that, and says so—often. The parents' eyes are apt to light up when they see a kids' novel about starting out in a new school, and how after weeks of loneliness fifth-grader Fred gets accepted. They may well get a copy for their own unhappy Kevin.

There's more. The parents may be trying to improve the child's character. In that case, instead of problem-books they will be giving virtue-books. In Victorian times a virtue-book was apt to stress honesty, hard work, obedience to one's parents. A current virtue-book, while certainly not discouraging honesty or hard work or even going to bed at the time set by one's parents, is more apt to stress sensitivity, caring, and openness to new experience. Concepcion comes from Guatemala, and at first she seems totally weird, but later she becomes Kate's best friend. That sort of thing.

There's more still. The parents may be thinking about literature, not life. They may want their child to have some sense of what good writing is. They then carefully avoid all the Nancy Drews and mutant turtle books. If it's mutation, they think of Pinocchio, or Arthur in *The Once and Future King*. If girl detectives—but they don't think about girl detectives. They think about Jo March and Mary Poppins and, not yet a Wilder, Miss Laura Ingalls.

The parents may even be thinking about themselves. If they've got any sense, and they expect to read so much as one chapter of the new book aloud, they certainly will consider themselves. They'll get a book that will interest them, too. Goodbye Nancy Drew.

Most of these goals do not conflict with each other. In fact, every now and then there's a book that combines practically all of them. Mary Stolz's *A Dog on Barkham Street* is such a one.

To begin with, it gives a child enormous pleasure. Probably it gives the most pleasure to a child who, like the main character, is a preadolescent boy, but I have also seen an adolescent girl reading it with delight: my daughter when she was fifteen.

The pleasure comes from many things. First, the book creates the wonderful, safe, snug feeling of a happy family. And it does so with utter truth. Edward Frost, the ten-year-old boy who's the main character, is both highly individual and a sort of epitome of boydom, down to his messy room. (It's messy in a special Edward way.) Mrs. Frost, his mother, has plenty of faults, including being a nag—a sweet-tempered one—and even more virtues. She is a delight to read about. Mr. Frost is a father one would like to have.

Then there's the plot. Edward's may be a happy family, but that doesn't mean nothing happens. On the first page of the book you learn that Edward has the misfortune to live next door to a boy two years older and very much bigger than him, a bully by temperament. No father and no mother can protect a child from humiliation by another child, though in this book both try.

On the eighth page of the book you learn that most of the time Edward isn't trying to escape the boy next door, he's wishing he had a dog. His mother has said no dog until he shows himself to be responsible about his room, his father's tools, etc. She wants him to be responsible about the dog, too, so *she* won't always be the one having to clean up after it and take it for walks.

On page 33 you learn that the uncle Edward has never seen is about to come for a visit. Edward has never met Uncle Josh because Josh is a hobo, a living testament to irresponsibility (and freedom). For the last ten years he's been out West, bumming around. When he does arrive for the visit, he has with him an altogether endearing dog named Argess.

These three elements of plot—the bully, the dog, and the uncle—work together in complex and unexpected ways, and produce the sort of book that children stay up late in bed to finish.

But the biggest source of pleasure is the style. Mary Stolz plays the English language the way Rostropovich plays the cello. She can make it do almost anything. That's easy for me to say; it's also easy for me to demonstrate. Consider just the first paragraph of the book, wherein the reader is plunged into Edward's life. Here is what Ms. Stolz writes:

> Edward Frost, who had his share of problems, didn't
> see how he'd ever solve the biggest one. This was
> Martin Hastings, the bully of Barkham Street. Mar-
> tin was two years older than Edward, and there was

no solution for this. Martin would continue to be two years older until he was a hundred and Edward was ninety-eight. Edward had a feeling that even then he might not be entirely safe.

If that last sentence doesn't fetch you, then you probably don't like stylish writing. Even then, you might enjoy the way Ms. Stolz combines adult and childish points of view in that sentence, clearly loving both. Even if *that* leaves you cold, you might admire how she has the story off and rolling in less than seventy-five words.

But enough about the elements of pleasure in this book. Now consider some of the other objectives a person might have in giving a book to a child, for instance, to encourage a currently nonreading child to read. I doubt if *A Dog on Barkham Street* is suitable for that. The language is clear, and even simple, but the thought is not.

How about for dealing with a problem? You bet. This book has a lot to say to any kid who has been bullied—and were any of them to read it, it has a lot to say to bullies, too. They might even come to understand what makes them do it.

Virtue? Yes, that's here, too. The deepest theme in the whole book is the question of responsibility. Edward, his friend Rod, Uncle Josh, Mrs. Frost, Mr. Frost, the dog Argess, a nameless railroad man, all contribute to that theme. Rostropovich is now conducting the orchestra. In no way is the book saying some simpleminded thing about do your duty and act responsibly; on the contrary, it's the very real lure of a life like Uncle Josh's that gives the book its force.

Good literature? Yes, of course. A pleasure for the parent to read aloud? If you're in any serious doubt, go back and read that first paragraph aloud right now. After that, you might want to go get a copy of the book.

A Dog on Barkham Street.
Mary Stolz. 1960.

❧ 6 ❧

Nathaniel's Wonder-Book

*T*HE YEAR 1851 was almost a miraculous one in American literature. There were only about a thousand books published in this country that year—a week's supply at current rates. But what a thousand! For example, in April, Nathaniel Hawthorne published *The House of the Seven Gables.* In June, Harriet Beecher Stowe began to serialize *Uncle Tom's Cabin.* And in October, Herman Melville brought out *Moby-Dick.*

All that was for adults. But then in November Hawthorne published again; the first really good book for children ever written by an American. It was called *A Wonder-Book for Boys and Girls,* and it consisted of six stories rather freely adapted from Greek mythology. The story of Perseus (who cut off the Gorgon's head) is there, and King Midas with his golden touch, and Baucis and Philemon, the old couple who are given the magic pitcher by Zeus himself. Hawthorne pretends that a quick-witted and inventive sophomore at Williams College named Eustace Bright is adapting the old Greek stories for an audience of his little cousins, as Ovid once adapted them for an audience of grown-up Romans.

Eustace's cousins—he has a full dozen of them, from kindergarten age up to about twelve—loved the stories, and so did the public. The book was a big success. The publishers rushed out a second printing in time for Christmas, and *that* did so well that in 1853 Hawthorne wrote a sequel that is even better than *A Wonder-Book*. Here Eustace (by now a college senior) tells six more stories. They include Jason's quest for the golden fleece, Cadmus planting the dragon's teeth, the whole adventure of Proserpina's abduction by Pluto, lord of the underworld, and her eventual if incomplete rescue. This book Hawthorne called *Tanglewood Tales*, because Eustace is supposedly telling them in a place in western Massachusetts called Tanglewood. (A real place, too. I think they play music there now.)

As Hawthorne freely admits, he took great liberties with Greek mythology. To give a small example, in classical versions Baucis and Philemon's magic pitcher pours wine. Really good wine. Baucis and her husband were Phrygian peasants, extremely poor, but as generous to strangers as most of their neighbors were inhospitable. One night two travelers come to their door, tired and hungry. They invite the strangers in, and share what supper they have, which is olives, cabbage, and a little bit of vinegary wine. This they dilute with water, so there will be seconds for the guests. They take none themselves—none, that is, until they perceive that the pitcher is not getting a bit lower, even after seconds and thirds. When they do finally taste it, they find it has become a rich and noble vintage. It's about then that they begin to realize that their two guests are gods in disguise.

Hawthorne keeps that situation—indeed, to my taste he makes it more interesting than it ever was in classical mythology, because he presents the psychology of realizing you are in the presence of immortal gods with such insight. But the menu! Those old Greeks now serve New England food. They have a little bit of bread and cheese to offer their guests . . . and a small pitcher of milk. For the next forty years they serve foaming glasses of milk to the kings and heroes and ordinary travelers who stop off at the marble palace Zeus and Hermes build for them. It's admirable, but it's not Greek.

Or to take a much larger example, Hawthorne strips almost all the sex out of classical mythology. Everyone who knows the story of the Minotaur will remember that Prince Theseus is able to kill this monster only because he is helped by King Minos's daughter Ariadne, who has fallen in love with him. When he and the other Athenians sail away from Crete, Ariadne is with them.

In Hawthorne's version, Ariadne still gives the essential help, but when Theseus urges her to come back to Athens with them, she gently declines: "'No, Theseus,' the maiden said . . . 'I cannot go with you. My father is old, and has nobody but myself to love him. Hard as you think his heart is, it would break to lose me.'" Hawthorne's tales are full of such tenderhearted fathers and mothers.

And Ariadne at least seems to be a grown young woman. Many of the classical heroines Hawthorne turns into children. Europa is just a little girl—a very pretty one—when Zeus in the form of a white bull swims off with her. Proserpina seems to be somewhere around eleven or twelve when Pluto abducts her, and though she is a lovely child, she's definitely not a nymphet. It isn't even quite clear whether Pluto wants to marry her when she gets a bit older, or whether he wants to adopt her as a daughter.

But then, sex is not the only adventure in the world. With a few unhappy exceptions, for children it's not even a possible one. There are other things to be interested in then, such as magic, and heroism, and treasure hunts (which is what many of the Greek myths are). Hawthorne is good on all of these, and particularly good on the magic. He handles it in about twenty different ways, and all of them are wonderful. He fills it with awe, as when Athena is present and invisibly performing a miracle. He makes it fanciful and a little comic, as when King Midas acquires the golden touch. As for Pegasus, the magical winged horse, here he gilds the account with a kind of glory that you will find very few places in literature. The account of the young hero Bellerophon riding Pegasus is perhaps more like the writing of Antoine de Saint-Exupéry in *Wind, Sand, and Stars* than anything else, even though Saint-Exupéry wrote about the early days of aviation from actual experience, and Hawthorne could only imagine what it would be like to soar up on a winged horse. He imagined well.

Hawthorne himself had no problem with making Philemon drink milk, or Hercules behave chastely around wood nymphs, or greedy King Midas (like cruel King Minos) be deeply devoted to an only child. The classical myths, he said, "are legitimate subjects for every age to clothe with its own garniture of manners and sentiment, and imbue with its morality." At least when they're such garniture and morality as his, I fully agree.

A Wonder-Book for Boys and Girls, 1851.
Tanglewood Tales, 1853.
Nathaniel Hawthorne.

❧ 7 ❧

Living Dolls II

*M*UCH OF THE best writing for children has been about small creatures who are surrounded by large ones. Since that pretty well describes how children themselves live, the appeal is a natural one.

Sometimes the small beings are animals and the large ones people, as in scores of mouse books, rabbit books, and mole books. Sometimes the small ones *are* people, and the larger ones some bigger race, like trolls, or the kind of giant that Jack killed. Sometimes the smaller creatures are fairies, elves, gnomes, dwarves, or hobbits, and the large ones men. Occasionally the small ones are miniature human beings—living dolls—and the large ones people of the usual size.

Probably the best example of this last genre (unless you count *Gulliver's Travels* itself, and you shouldn't, because it wasn't written for children) is *Mistress Masham's Repose*. T. H. White published that small gem in 1946. In it, a colony of Lilliputians that was brought back to England in Swift's time eventually escaped, and has been living for many generations on an island in a lake on a ducal estate. An orphaned little girl of the ducal family and a wicked clergyman rediscover the colony more or less simultaneously, and sharp adventures follow. You'll hear more about them a few chapters hence.

Much cozier and perhaps a little cuter than White, but really just as good, is Mary Norton's series of books about the tiny people called Borrowers. She may be cozy, in a Dorothy Sayers–Miss Reade–Lord Peter Wimsey sort of way, but she entirely avoids White's gruff sentimentality. She is fully his equal at adventures.

White, of course, got his idea directly from Jonathan Swift. Norton got hers from her own childhood. Born in 1903, she lived her early years in that golden moment in English history, the ten years just after the Victorian age and just before World War I. "In those days," she once explained, "one would buy small, china dolls with moveable arms and flaxen hair, naked except for shoes and socks, which were painted on. They stood about three or four inches high, and were for sale among the lollipops in every village store."

Norton acquired a considerable number of these dolls. She made clothes for them and then began to use them as actors in complicated dramas. Only instead of making them surrogates for full-sized human beings, as millions of little girls have done, she kept them their actual size, and peopled her parents' garden with four-inch adults and three-inch children. She imagined "small fearful people picking their way through miniature growth," living in what she called "a tiny Eden."

Later, as a grown-up, reimagining the small people, she enlarged them just slightly (an adult Borrower is five or six inches tall) and moved them into human houses. There they live secret lives, mostly under the floors, in well-built apartments they construct with miniature tools. Everything they need they steal from what they call human beans. Food, of course. But also teacups from dollhouses, thimbles, candle ends, handkerchiefs (they make good bedsheets), even a small pocket watch to use as a big clock on the wall. That's the reason we human beans so often can't find things. The Borrowers have borrowed them—they never call it stealing.

The Borrowers, which is the first of six books about these small creatures (all six are good) centers on a family who live under the floor in an old manor house in the peaceful village of Little Fordham. The time, of course, is the golden moment, just before World War I, horses and candles and gaslight still thriving.

Borrowers speak the same language as the larger people whose culture they share, except they are a little sloppy. They use a slightly mangled version of lower-class rural English speech, complete with the pithiness. It makes good reading. Even their names tend to be slight corruptions of human ones. The family under the floor in the manor house consists of Pod, the provident father; Homily, the thrifty and overprotective mother; and Arrietty, their altogether en-chanting five-inch-tall daughter. On the fringes of the book are other Borrowers, such as Uncle Hendreary, his rash daughter Eggletina, and the upper-class young man Pere-grine—who being gentry has got his name right. (The other Borrowers instantly corrupt it; they call him Peagreen.)

As the story begins, Arrietty is rolling a potato, half as high as she is, into the kitchen. Homily means to cut some slices off to cook for dinner. She has a woodstove made of an old cogwheel; the fuel is candle grease and twigs. No smoke to give their location away.

Soon her father returns with his borrowing bag from an expedition upstairs. He looks pale and frightened. After Ar-rietty has gone to bed, Homily demands to know what's the matter. Pod stares at her gloomily. "I been 'seen,'" he says.

To be seen by a human bean is one of the worst things that can happen to a Borrower. The big people are apt to want to catch the little ones and put them in cages, or even to set a cat on them, as if they were mice. Pod was climbing up a curtain when he was spotted by a nine-year-old boy who had just arrived in the manor house on a visit. He could easily have been caught, but the boy chose to let him go.

Arrietty hears the whole story the next day, and this

narrow escape of her father's should make her more willing
to stay uncomplainingly under the floor. It doesn't. It
makes her even wilder to get out. "No one to talk to," she
laments, "no one to play with, nothing to see but dust and
passages . . ."

Arrietty does go out borrowing with her father, and she
not only is seen, she comes to be almost friends with the
human boy, who is pretty short on playmates himself. Eventually she gets into the worst of all plights for a Borrower.
How she gets out again, with the boy's help, is the main
story of the book.

I should warn anyone who buys *The Borrowers* to give or
to read to a small human bean that the first chapter is the
weakest. You have to read it because it contains essential
information and also because it sets things up for the last
chapter, but it's slow going. Don't be put off. The wonderful
story begins with chapter 2.

I should also mention two or three more things that
make it wonderful. One is the completely believable psychology of the Borrowers. Unlike elves and so forth, they
have no magic or special powers of any kind—they have to
get on unaided, just as we do. Unlike all human beans except small children, they are pleasingly free of conscience.
They are intellectually simple, emotionally complex, and
utterly delightful.

Another is the consistent ingenuity with which they turn
human artifacts to their own purposes. It's the same pleasure one gets in watching Robinson Crusoe set up house-
keeping with what he can salvage from the wrecked ship,
but intensified from the tiny scale.

Finally, there is an element contributed not by Mary
Norton but by Beth and Joe Krush, who drew the twenty-
three illustrations. They illustrated all the Borrower books,
and each is a visual joy. What the Krushes have produced
are sort of Dickensian miniatures, but without the touch of
caricature. Arrietty herself is the best of all, pretty, daring

creature that she is. In fact, it is a little frustrating to find oneself feeling fatherly about a girl who is five inches tall and lives under the kitchen floor in a house in an English village in 1911.

The only solution is to read the book aloud to some small human bean.

The Borrowers.
Mary Norton. 1952.

❧ 8 ❧

A Black Planet

HIDDEN IN THE basement of a New York public school, behind a false wall, there's a working model of the solar system: an orrery. Mr. Pool, once a teacher but now the janitor of this school, holds secret classes in that room for a small but very select group. There are two kids in his astronomy class. One is a homeless boy named Buddy Clark, a dropout from the eighth grade. The other, an overprotected fat boy called Junior Brown, is a musical prodigy—and also a world-class neurotic.

Class is in session at the moment the book begins. The reader enters the hidden room, lit only by the faintly glowing sun and planets of what does not quite resemble our usual solar system. There's a reason for that. Mr. Pool and Buddy, who built the orrery together, have just added a new element: a very large planet that shares Earth's orbit. This new planet they have named Junior Brown.

Junior the boy watches in mingled delight and disbelief as Junior the planet follows tiny Earth around the sun. Then skepticism triumphs. "'It couldn't happen,' Junior said, shaking his head. 'That close, the earth wouldn't be nothing but a pockmark on the planet of Junior Brown.'" But Mr. Pool and Buddy counter with a quick story about asteroids and nodal points. Junior half-believes again. It is a funny and touching scene.

The day it occurs happens to be a Friday. That's also the day Junior gets his weekly piano lesson down on West 78th Street, and he has to leave the room with the orrery early. He feels around in the dark for his Fake Book, finds it, stands up to go.

Fake Book? What's that?

> In no way false, the Fake Book was a thick volume of
> jazz and rock tunes arranged and copied profession-
> ally and in keys suitable for the average singer. The
> book had cost Junior's mother fifty dollars. Junior al-
> ways carried the book although he never used the
> arrangements. But hidden inside were his music
> lessons and his own classical compositions.

By now the reader is beginning to think that *The Planet of Junior Brown* is one of those books about a bunch of lov-able eccentrics—excuse me, lovable *talented* eccentrics—and the reader is right. Junior, for all his gross overweight, is a deeply appealing character, and at least part genius. Buddy, the homeless boy, is so bright and so crazy in a nice way as to be irresistible. Miss Lynora Peebs, Junior's piano teacher, is weird and charming, too. She's somewhere in her fifties, but looks thirty-nine. She was once a concert pianist; now she almost never leaves the big apartment on West 78th Street, its rooms bursting with all the antique furni-ture, junk, old newspapers, and so on she has got in there. Not to mention the imaginary relative who lives with her.

But, as you soon discover, this comedy of eccentrics is only one level, the top one. *Planet* is an extraordinarily deep and ambitious kids' book. It has two other levels, and on them it is not comic at all.

The perceptive reader may have noticed by now that all these characters are black. (Well, not Miss Peebs. She's light brown, "with a yellowish tint glowing through a girlish smoothness.") On the second level, almost all the comic/

eccentric details apply quite seriously to black life in America. Consider the hidden room with the orrery. Consider Junior's Fake Book. Both are themselves, of course: real things in the book. Both also symbolize aspects of deep black consciousness (and, indeed, deep human consciousness), under all the stereotypes.

The other planets in the book do this also: the planets of Buddy Clark. These are not whimsical additions to an orrery; these are hidden groups of homeless black kids in abandoned buildings. Each of these planets has a leader who is also the food provider and the educator. In two of these planets, at different times in the book, the leader is Buddy Clark. Even as he himself is under the tutelage of Mr. Pool, he has younger kids under his. The whole system is quite separate from official American society, welfare, etc. And it is not a system of coping, it is a system of growth. On this second level the book is strong and hopeful.

Finally, there is the scary third level. Here eccentricity is very close indeed to madness. Take Miss Peebs's imaginary relative who lives with her. In a book that was just cute and lovable, he would be some harmless old coot. Not this fellow. She has imagined someone dangerous and diseased. There is a notable scene where Junior persuades her he can take this creature down in the elevator—and when he does, the creature becomes real for him. And not funnily, but scarily. On this level, the book is about the kinds of wounds that almost all human beings have, suffer from, must live with.

Because of the third level, *The Planet of Junior Brown* is not a book to give to just any kid. It is powerful medicine. And at times it drops plausibility and even story line in favor of symbolic depth. Strong and thoughtful kids will do best with it.

And yet . . . it is also such a funny, charming book that I hate to say anything that might limit its audience. There's a scene, for example, where Junior is telling Buddy how he

spent the preceding evening. His mother had dragged him
to a Weight Watchers meeting. Buddy plays straight man
while Junior explains what Weight Watchers do at their
meetings:

> "They talked a lot about celery and raw mushrooms."
> "Gawd," Buddy said.
> "They seem to think pretty highly of broiled fish."
> "Nobody eat that stuff," Buddy said.

If you find Junior's way of approaching broiled fish even
nearly as funny as I do, you may find you can't resist reading
The Planet of Junior Brown yourself, and then maybe giving
it to an imaginative twelve or fourteen year old.

> *The Planet of Junior Brown.*
> Virginia Hamilton. 1971.

❧ 9 ❧

The Freedom of the Woods

FOR THE LAST 130 years or so, small boys in America have played the game called cowboys and Indians. Even now, in the age of Nintendo and Native Americans, they continue to play it.

The curious thing is that nearly all the small boys want to be Indians. When I was little myself, I used to pretend I *was* part Indian. My father had a framed portrait of a Blackfoot Indian boy named First Stabber, and it was my favorite piece of artwork in the world. First Stabber looked to be about twelve. He was dressed in fringed buckskin; he wore beautifully beaded moccasins; in one hand he held a lethal-looking hatchet and in the other a hunting knife. I knew I could never be as good as that—but I nevertheless often pretended that I was his younger brother. When I was about eight, I even tried asking my mother to call me Second Stabber, but this did not appeal to her.

It is easy to see why being Indian appeals to small boys, though. At least as they imagine Indian life in the days before whites came, it was wonderfully free and daring. Better yet, most of it was on a technological level that a boy can imagine mastering. There's no way he can manufacture caps and cap pistols for himself (much less fix his Nintendo, if there's a circuitry problem), but he really could make himself a bow and a set of arrows. Condos are beyond his reach, but a tipi is not. If he were an Indian, a boy of twelve or fourteen might perfectly conceivably be able to feed, clothe, and house himself in the woods, and thus—at least for a summer weekend—be entirely independent of dull parental life.

There is one book above all others that will appeal to the boys (and girls) who have had such fantasies. And it is quite capable of creating the fantasy in those who haven't. This is Ernest Thompson Seton's *Two Little Savages.*

The book takes place in Canada, but not in one of the wild parts. It's set in tame farm country, where deer are extinct and Indians have long been gone. The nearest thing to wilderness is a big swamp ten miles away where no one lives because no one has gotten around to draining the water yet. The time must be around 1880.

The main character is a boy named Yan. Yan is no farm kid; he has grown up in a small provincial city, one of the many children in a shabby-genteel family.

Yan is the family misfit. What he cares about is pure nature. He dreams—what else?—about being an Indian, and in his secret fantasies he tries to talk and act like one. What his parents and most of his siblings care about is respectability, plus a particularly deadening kind of religion. When Yan tries to get a dollar together to buy his first nature book—he's about eleven—he starts doing odd jobs for neighbors to earn a nickel here, a dime there. His father finds out, and instantly forbids him to continue. Stacking firewood is not work fit for a gentleman's son, the father thunders. But this same father gives him no allowance at all, not even a nickel a week. Says he can't afford to.

When Yan is fourteen he gets tuberculosis, and is sent off to live on a farm for a year to regain his health. He will earn every penny of his room and board by doing farm chores, so this his father can afford.

William Raften, the Irish-born farmer who takes Yan in, has a son the same age, a boy named Sam. Sam shares Yan's passion for the woods, and quickly gets infected with his equal passion to live like an Indian. Before Yan has been a week on the farm, the two boys have started to build a tipi in the patch of woods down by the creek that runs through Raften's farm. The farmer is perfectly willing to let them, provided they get all their chores done first.

They hit a problem almost immediately. They are trying to fasten the tipi poles together with willow withes, which keep slipping. The farmer comes down to see how his son and the city boy are doing, and offers them some baling wire from the barn. Yan answers:

> "We ain't allowed to use anything but what the Indi-
> ans had or could get in the woods."
>   "An' who don't allow yez?"
>   "The rules."

Mr. Raften is amused by this, and promptly shows them how to find and use the tough branches of a shrub called leatherwood.

Yan and Sam soon have their tipi and their camp. They now constitute themselves the Sanger Indians. Sam Raften has metamorphosed into the Great Chief Woodpecker, and Yan is the almost as great Chief Little Beaver. And the book is fully launched.

A long series of adventures follow. Woodpecker and Lit-tle Beaver learn to paint themselves with war paint. They learn to make arrows, to hunt, to track, to read the forest floor like a book. They encounter an imaginary banshee and a horribly real three-fingered tramp. With help from Mrs. Raften, they get permission to spend three weeks entirely in the woods, extra chores to be done when they get back. They admit a third boy to the tribe. They get a technical ad-viser in the person of a lonely old man named Caleb Clark, who many years ago had lived with real Indians. There's a grand climax, involving a trip to the big swamp, a new and rival "Indian" tribe, and the three-fingered tramp.

Two Little Savages has some four or five separate charms. The greatest, of course, is the wonderful if vicarious sense of accomplishment the reader gets while watching Yan and Sam acquire skill after skill. But it isn't entirely vicarious. Seton is unobtrusive about his instruction, but relying only on *Two Little Savages,* a reader could fletch his or her own arrows, make a very beautiful wood and leather drum, or build an excellent small dam. All this using only what the Indians had or could get in the woods.

But the book offers other pleasures almost as great. The character studies of Yan and Sam, for example, and of many other people as well, such as Guy Burns, the irrepressibly boastful third member of the tribe. There are the marginal illustrations, by my count numbering well over two hundred. My two favorites are a study of twelve-year-old Guy Burns with and without war paint (the difference is amazing), and a tiny set of a dozen tipis as decorated by different tribes. Seton, a master artist, drew all these himself.

Then there's Seton's ability to keep two or three plots going at once, all of them exciting. There are the formal full-page illustrations (twenty-two of them); there is Sam's lively wit; and so on.

I can think of only two flaws. Seton does have a certain taste for melodrama when dealing with grown-up characters. And in true Victorian style, he is impossibly sentimental about little girls. But there is only one of these in the book—Sam's kid sister Minnie–and only one scene where you actually cringe.

I can never be First Stabber (and now that as a grown-up I know what the name means, I wouldn't want to be). But maybe I can be that milder thing, First Recommender. I'll recommend. *Two Little Savages* would make a stunning present for almost any kid who loves the woods.

Two Little Savages.
Ernest Thompson Seton. 1902.

✺ *10* ✺

Living Dolls III

WHEN PEOPLE GET really caught up in a book, they often find themselves reluctant to reach the end. They wonder what the characters would be doing if the author had only let them have a few more chapters. If writers themselves, they may go beyond wondering. They may take over the characters, and give them space in their own books. They may even take over the plot, and write an actual sequel.

T. H. White, the distinguished author of *The Once and Future King,* was devoted to both practices. As a very young man, he tried continuing Jane Austen in a special White-ish way. Like most of us, he loved *Pride and Prejudice.* So he wrote . . . not a novel about the married life of Elizabeth Bennet and Mr. Darcy as it would have occurred between 1797 and about 1840, but a twentieth-century murder mystery, set partly on Darcy's estate. Many of the characters are descendents of Elizabeth and Darcy. That book is called *Darkness at Pemberley.*

A few years later, he introduced two characters from a Robert Surtees novel into a hunting novel of his own. Since Surtees wrote between 1838 and 1864, his characters would now be quite elderly. No problem. White has them holed up in a sort of large wine cellar. It's the wine that keeps them going.

White also did a bit of rescue work on Robert Louis Stevenson, and at one time he considered bringing Don Quixote into the twentieth century. (Graham Greene later had the same thought, and wrote *Father Quixote*.)

But the best continuation White ever did was in a children's book. He continued *Gulliver's Travels*. He does not pick up where Swift left off, he merely picks up one of Swift's hints.

Readers of *Gulliver* may remember that when that intrepid mariner leaves Lilliput, he takes with him a pocketful of Lilliputian farm animals. He's got a little flock of three-inch-long sheep and half a dozen cows the size of chipmunks. These he shows to the captain of the ship that rescues him—in fact, he gives Captain Biddel one of each.

At this point White takes over. In Swift, Captain Biddel now fades from view. In White he steps forward, a look of greed on his face. A shrewd businessman, Captain Biddel realizes there's big money to be made out of tiny farm animals—and even bigger money to be made out of tiny human beings. The first chance he gets, he sails back to the latitude where he picked Gulliver up. He cruises around until he finds Blefescu and Lilliput. He then kidnaps thirteen people, plus as many sheep, cows, and thumb-sized sheepdogs as he can grab, and sails home to England. Here he exhibits his captives in a sort of miniature traveling zoo.

After much suffering, the Lilliputians escape with their animals. They manage to get to a small island in a lake on a country estate, where they hide. Two hundred years later, their descendents are still living on that island, nearly a thousand of them by now: the nation of Lilliput in Exile. How have they escaped detection, right up to the year 1946? Partly by taking extraordinary care, partly through good fortune. It is their good luck that the estate, a ducal one, is both vast and neglected. The lake is choked with water weeds, the island overgrown with briars. No full-sized human being has set foot there in many years.

All that is background. The story White tells begins
when a full-sized person does come. She is the heroine of
the book and the heiress to the estate, a ten-year-old girl
named Maria. Do not imagine some privileged little future
duchess. Yes, Maria will be a great lady some day. Right
now she is an orphan, left in the guardianship of the local
vicar, an odious man. This cleric, the Rev. Mr. Hater, has
appointed a remote cousin of Maria's, a Miss Brown, to be
her governess. Miss Brown is worse than odious, she is
cruel. She and the vicar keep Maria rigidly suppressed; they
also siphon off most of what little money still comes in, so
that the great house of Malplaquet gradually continues to
crumble. Maria's only friends are the one servant left from
her parents' time, who is the cook, and a remarkably eccentric professor who occupies a gamekeeper's cottage elsewhere on the estate.

Maria, having no parents to love or be loved by, not allowed even to keep a pet, is naturally thrilled when she dis-
covers Lilliput in Exile—and her first act is to steal a baby
that she finds asleep in a two-inch cradle. She intends to
take it home and keep it (well hidden from Miss Brown) as
something to play with and to lavish affection on. When the
mother attempts to prevent this, Maria takes her, too. Then
she is both puzzled and angry that mother and baby are not
grateful at being carried back to the palace of Malplaquet
and offered bits of a strawberry. She would have been so
nice to them!

Part of the action of the book turns on Maria's discovery
that ownership and love do not go well together. Suppose,
the Professor says to Maria, you become the patroness of
Lilliput in Exile, their Superwoman, their strong protector:
"You would be a Big Bug then, however kind you were, and
they would be little bugs, without the capitals. They would
come to depend on you; you would come to boss them.
They would get servile, and you would get lordly." We who

live in a Big Bug nation should recognize that description. And maybe wince a little when we think of all the Lilliputs we currently boss—and expect to be loved by.

Maria does learn her lesson, and does become friends with the Lilliputians on an equal basis. They then open their hidden city to her, and share their lives. The best chapters of the book result, as Maria gets to see how these tiny people operate in a world where a robin on the grass can look them in the eye, a domestic cat looms larger than ever a saber-toothed tiger did to the cave people, a swooping owl means instant death. My very favorite describes the fishing expedition she gets to watch. The People keep a square-rigged sailing ship in a secret harbor on the far side of the island, and at night they sail out to hunt pike rather the way Nantucketers used to sail out to hunt whales.

But eventually Miss Brown catches Maria sneaking out to go visit the island—and worse, she then finds several tiny presents the People have given her. Maria refuses to explain where she got these things. When Miss Brown locks Maria in her room, planning to starve her into submission, the People eventually come in force, about five hundred of them, to bring her food. (Three whole roasted bullocks, forty-eight loaves of grass-seed bread.)

The worst possible thing then happens. Miss Brown catches a Lilliputian. She and the Vicar realize, far more clearly and ruthlessly than Captain Biddel did in the eighteenth century, that the owner of a lot of miniature human beings can get very rich indeed. A thrilling struggle ensues, with Maria, the People, the Cook, and the Professor on one side, and the Vicar and Miss Brown on the other. The People eventually win.

T. H. White was a good and possibly a great writer. Like most such, he was prepared to take almost infinite pains. *Mistress Masham's Repose* went through four radically different versions between the time White began to write it in

1942 and its publication in 1946. In the first version, for example, the Vicar and Miss Brown speak in Elizabethan blank verse.

But even the fourth version, the one that finally got printed, is not quite as good as it might have been. White was in deep grief at the time he finished it, almost incapacitated. "I lost the only living creature I loved on the 25th of last November," he wrote sadly in 1945, "and I know that I shall call out her name when I die." Polishing the manuscript with a cool head seemed out of the question. So he sent it to his best friend, the novelist David Garnett, with instructions to edit it freely: "You may leave out whole chapters, if you like, for I trust your taste implicitly and my own not at all."

Garnett cut no chapters, but he did write T. H. White a memorable letter. It is part gasp of pleasure and part solemn warning.

"You have stumbled upon a most beautiful subject which you will never get again & you have the opportunity to write a masterpiece," Garnett said. Some of that masterpiece is already present, he went on, but much of the book is spoiled by facetious and tiresome jokes, by "a lot of twaddle about Miss Pribble [as Miss Brown then was] and the Vicar," and so on. Plus an overindulgence in capital letters when the Lilliputians are talking, I'd add.

"It is a real tragedy," Garnett concluded, "for you are on the edge of a book which will make you immortal." He begged White to delay publication and to revise still more.

White listened to what his friend said, and he did make extensive new changes. They are not extensive enough. It was *The Once and Future King* that would make White immortal, not *Mistress Masham's Repose*.

And yet, as finally issued, it *is* a masterpiece, though a flawed one. I can think of few greater pleasures in reading aloud to a bookish child than to read that child first *Gulliver's Travels* and then *Mistress Masham* right after. If the child happens to be especially observant, he or she may notice that Swift uses the Lilliputians (*and* the Brobdignagians *and* the Yahoos) to belittle human nature, but White uses them to magnify it. It is a stunning book for a child to know.

Mistress Masham's Repose.
T. H. White. 1946.

✦ 11 ✦

Three Fine Mice

IT IS HISTORIC FACT that prisoners, especially in earlier days when prisons lacked TV, libraries, visiting hours, etc., depended heavily on animal companionship. A mouse scavenging for crumbs, a bird lighting at a barred outside window, even a spider catching flies in a corner—these gave the lonely prisoner something to watch and maybe a fellow creature to love.

This fact, greatly amplified, is the genesis of Margery Sharp's nine books about the elegant white mouse Miss Bianca and her indomitable if slightly shaggy admirer Bernard. *The Rescuers,* the first and best-known of the nine books, opens at a general meeting of the Mouse Prisoners' Aid Society branch in the capital of an unnamed Mediterranean country. It is customary for members of the Society to volunteer for jail duty, going off to companion some poor wretch in solitary confinement. An innocent wretch, a political prisoner usually, though sometimes criminals, too. Principal companion duties: to pretend to be delighted with the stale crumbs from the prisoner's bread, perhaps in time to run up his ragged pant leg, and to submit to being petted. The mice do comfort work, in short. They have never tried to help a prisoner actually escape—what could a creature weighing two ounces do against iron bars? And it's only male mice who even do the comforting. The Ladies' Guild

of the Society has as *its* chief duty the preparation of re-
freshments for the meetings.

That's about to change. The Ladies' Guild may never
have sent a volunteer off to prison, but its members do vote,
and they have recently helped to elect the first female
mouse ever to chair this branch of the Society. She is a
mouse with big ideas. She wants to stage a rescue.

What has led her to this desire is the news that in her
country's worst and darkest prison, a Norwegian poet lan-
guishes. Like many of Margery Sharp's mice, she profoundly admires poets, especially those, like Robert Burns
and Sir John Suckling, who have brought mice into their
poetry. (*Her feet beneath her petticoat / Like little mice stole
in and out.* Suckling, 1646.) She instantly vows to get this
young Norwegian out.

But how? She will not be able to do it herself. She's bold
enough, but she's also middle aged, verging on elderly, and
simply not up to the rigorous trip to the Black Castle, let
alone getting past the Head Jailer's cat. That legendary
killer, "twice natural size and four times as fierce," as they
know from the one member of the Society who has actually
been to the Black Castle, has never yet let a mouse reach
the cells.

Furthermore, a mouse that speaks Norwegian is essential to the enterprise. Getting past the demon cat, mapping
out an escape route, somehow obtaining the jailer's keys,
will not be enough. The rescuer must be able to communi-
cate with the poet. Madam Chairwoman speaks not a word
of Norwegian.

What she tells the appalled general meeting is that (1)
there is a jailed poet in the Black Castle, (2) they must free
him, and (3) first they must send an emissary to Norway to
find a volunteer. It's too much! She is almost voted down.

But then she reminds them of Miss Bianca, a beautiful
and aristocratic white mouse all of them have heard of and
none of them have met. Miss Bianca is the pet mouse of

the young son of the British ambassador to this nameless country. She lives in a porcelain pagoda in the embassy, and does not mingle with common mice. She does mingle with ambassadors. She has access to the diplomatic pouches. She will fly to Norway. If they can persuade her to, that is. And a member of the Society named Bernard does persuade her to, falling madly in love with her in the process.

In the end, three mice set out for the Black Castle: Miss Bianca, who has come back from Norway by tramp steamer with the volunteer, a hardy seafaring mouse named Nils; Bernard, low-born but heroic, holder of the Tybalt Star for gallantry in the face of cats; and, of course, Nils himself. After terrific adventures—most terrific of all with Mamelouke, the huge, sadistic cat—three mice and a poet return.

There are several reasons why this book and its successors are such fun to read. One is the sheer inventiveness of the plot. Ms. Sharp has a vivid imagination. She also has the same superb disdain for statistical probability that most small children themselves have. One example will suffice. When Miss Bianca and Nils reach the nameless country and get off the steamer ("they had been among the first to disembark"), they still have a long journey to the capital.

Miss Bianca, used to the diplomatic life, where competent underlings handle these details, doesn't even know in which direction the capital lies. Nils doesn't either, though, sea-lover that he is, he takes it for granted that if they follow the nearest river upstream, they will sooner or later get to the capital and even precisely to the British embassy. He just needs a boat.

And almost immediately they find one, bobbing by the pier. It's a seafaring mouse's dream. A model speedboat, about fifteen inches long, incredibly fast, this vessel is nuclear powered. It can easily take them a hundred miles upriver—or bring Nils back to Oslo, for that matter.

This boat is in fact the long-missing craft given to the ambassador's little son by the American naval attache. How did it find its way to the seaport at just the right moment? Could a boat that size avoid getting swamped by the first serious wave to come along? Stupid boring questions. Don't ask them, and also don't ask if you could really adapt nuclear propulsion to a boat one foot and three inches long. This is a world in which things happen as they should happen.

A related pair of delights are the sheer bubbling-over villainy of the villains, and the magnanimity with which the heroic characters such as Miss Bianca respond. Magnanimous means literally "great-souled," and these little mice are. Take Miss Bianca's first encounter with Mamelouke, the Head Jailer's cat.

Hitherto Miss B has known only one cat, a white Persian at the embassy, an aristocrat like herself. Apart from the ambassador's son, he was her dearest friend. For his sake she is prepared to like—and to trust—all cats. Thus when Mamelouke finally gets a chance to talk to her alone (Nils and Bernard are out on a castle ledge), he easily persuades her to come out from the mouse hole into an open room. She thinks he is inviting her to a game, as indeed he is—the traditional cat-and-mouse game that ends with the mouse's death. Miss B, of course, is fearless, both while she still believes in his benevolence and after she realizes that he intends to kill her. It's exhilarating to see how by a mixture of quick-wittedness and true courtesy she (temporarily) disarms him.

But the biggest delight of all is Margery Sharp's style. She writes with ease and freedom—but also with a strong touch of eighteenth-century elegance and an equally strong relish of twentieth-century irony. Few children, perhaps none, will recognize the eighteenth-century-ness for what it is (they may spot the irony), but all who are sensitive to language will know that something is going on, something more formal and shapely than they are used to. Such children will be enchanted with the way Miss Bianca talks, may begin themselves to talk a little that way. They will even relish the short poems she composes from time to time. These are full of eighteenth-century contractions like "e'er" and eighteenth-century apostrophes like "Dear Boy! I would not have thee weep!" Ms. Sharp is affectionately mocking the older century.

Children who are *not* sensitive to language will miss a great deal that goes on in the Miss Bianca books, and probably shouldn't be given them. I say only "probably," because sometimes the right book at the right moment will sensitize a childish ear—or, more accurately, wake a sleeping part of the brain. One of my two godsons, a boy devoted to facts, read *The Rescuers,* simply because it was around the house. At first he felt outraged by the liberties Margery Sharp takes, then amused, and finally, having read all her books, he became almost proprietary.

There is also a class of children who have missed practically everything. These are kids who have seen the Disney animated film called *The Rescuers,* and who suppose they have had an experience comparable to reading the book. They haven't. Oh, there are two mice in the movie who bear the names Bernard and Miss Bianca, and who are this far true to the book characters: one of them is male and the other female.

There is also a rescue in the movie—not of a Norwegian poet in a nameless Mediterranean country, but of an American orphan named Penny, in Florida. Quite an exciting rescue: the two alligators who guard her are an especial success. There is also a cat in the movie; he makes a splendid symbol of how great the difference between film and novel is. Mamelouke, you will recall, is a villain, treated both playfully and as real danger. The cat in the movie is a sentimental old feline with a white mustache, who has this to say: "Faith is a bluebird you see from afar." Mamelouke would throw up at that. Miss Bianca is too well-bred to react so physically (she does faint sometimes in true eighteenth-century style), but she would shrug her velvet shoulders, and suggest that it might be time to leave the movie theater.

Let me be fair. Disney never claimed that the movie had much to do with the book. What it says in the credits is that the film was "suggested" by the book. And that is clearly true. Even Penny, the tear-jerking little orphan, was suggested by Patience, the somewhat subtler child captive in a later Miss Bianca book. I'm not attacking the movie, or not very hard. It's actually quite funny when it isn't being gooey and sentimental. What I'm attacking is the widespread delusion that it gives you an experience on the level of the book. As if a huge can of Sprite equaled champagne.

There is, I think, a general truth about movies made from children's books. Three times out of four the book gets cheapened, or even lost. There are a few glorious exceptions, like *The Wizard of Oz* and *Bambi*. The movie *Wizard* is actually better than the book, and the movie *Bambi* is certainly equal to the book.

But more typical cases would be the two books that were my control group in the preface: *Charlotte's Web* and *The Hobbit*. Both have been made into movies; both suffered terribly in the process. One was cheapened, the other lost.

But I am a book person. Don't take my word for it. Trust instead the editors of the annual reference book called *Video Movie Guide*. They have ranked about twenty thousand movies, employing the familiar star system. A great movie gets five stars, a very good one four stars, and so on down. *Bambi* and *The Wizard* duly get their five. What of *Charlotte's Web?* Two stars, which is the lowest you can get and have any stars at all. The only lower rating is that insulting symbol a turkey. As children's book, *Charlotte* is one of the best we have. As movie, say these movie experts, it is "a vacuous musical."

How about *The Hobbit?* Also two stars. "Disappointing," say the cinema experts. Two stars also to the movie made from *Alice in Wonderland*; it is "long and boring."

Now *The Rescuers*, I admit, does better. It gets four stars, presumably because the video people are so taken with those alligators and with the comic albatross. I'll even concede that it deserves two and a half, or even three. It's just no substitute for Ms. Sharp.

Back to the bookshelf, friends.

The Rescuers.
Margery Sharp. 1959.

⊸ 12 ⊸

Two Magical Books

ORTY YEARS AGO in England, a late-blooming
children's writer named Lucy Boston published her
first book. Ms. Boston was sixty-two when *The
Children of Green Knowe* came out, and she had already led
several lives. She had dropped out of Oxford to be an army
nurse in World War I. While in France, she had married an
RAF pilot. When the marriage broke up, she became a
painter, and went to live in Italy. When World War II drove
her out, she returned to England and bought an eight-
hundred-year-old house near Cambridge. She then spent
many years returning it to its original twelfth-century state.
Owning that house led to her book.

Forty years ago in the United States, another late-
blooming children's writer published a book—not his first,
but his first really good one. Edward Eager was forty-three
when *Half Magic* came out. He had already lived a lot. He
had dropped out of Harvard to write plays, having already
written one as an undergraduate that was so successful that
he was able to live for some time on the royalties. When he
turned out not to be a major playwright, he drifted into the
then-new world of television, and discovered he had a talent for adapting grand operas so as to make them suffi-
ciently ungrand for small screens. He had married, become
a father, gotten passionately fond of reading aloud to his

son. While doing so, he first encountered the classic children's writer E. Nesbit. That encounter led to this book.

The Children of Green Knowe and *Half Magic* have more in common than being very good books by authors who started late. The important thing they have in common is magic itself. One has solemn magic, and the other has a more playful kind, but both are able, in the most literal sense, to hold children spellbound.

The Children of Green Knowe has the solemn magic. As it begins, a little boy named Tolly is traveling alone through the flooded fen country of England. He's on his way to spend a school vacation with his great-grandmother, who lives alone in an old, old house that's more like a castle. His father and his not-especially-nice stepmother are off working in Burma, and that's why he's to go stay with Mrs. Oldknow, whom he has never met.

The magic at Green Knowe—and there's a lot of it—is almost entirely linked with the past. Some of it is scary. For example, the somewhat run-down gardens contain a lot of topiary: a peacock, a squirrel, a deer, all clipped out of living yew trees. There's also a topiary man, huge and blind and menacing. This figure is known in the neighborhood as Green Noah. He was clipped out 120 years ago by the grandfather of old Boggis, the present aged gardener. Soon after, he had a curse put on him by a gypsy woman named Petronella. Tolly's four-times great-grandfather, Sir Toseland Oldknow, sitting as a judge, had sent Petronella's son to jail. The green man has not been clipped in many years, but this just makes him look wilder and more dangerous. Though rooted to the spot, he is probably able to grab.

Some of the enchantment is reassuring, like the great stone St. Christopher who has stood for hundreds of years against one wall of the house, and who once a year *can* move. At least there are people who think they have seen him outside the old church in Penny Soaky on Christmas Eve.

But most of the magic is ancient and sad and beautiful.

Tolly's favorite picture in his great-grandmother's house is of three children dressed in seventeenth-century fashion, together with their pretty young mother, and a grandmother dressed in black.

Even now, three hundred years later, various toys that those children had are stored in a box up in a high room that you reach by a winding stair. Tolly plays with some of those toys himself. And he comes gradually to think he can hear the voices of the three children.

Then he learns why. These long-ago relatives never ceased to be children. They and their mother all died within a few hours of each other, during the Great Plague, and Green Knowe has been more or less benevolently haunted by them ever since. Tolly's first meeting with his dead cousins is something to bring tears to the eyes. And also joy to the heart.

Half Magic is in a lighter mood altogether. It takes place in Toledo, Ohio, in the early 1920s. There is a really nice family consisting of four children and their mother. The mother works on a Toledo newspaper, making just enough money to scrape by. It's summer, but there is no way she can afford a lakefront cottage or anything like that. So how are Jane, Mark, Katharine, and Martha spending their days? Reading, mostly. One good thing about the Toledo library was that in the summer you could check out ten books at a time, instead of winter's measly three.

By chance they take out one of E. Nesbit's stories about four English children who have magic adventures. Like Edward Eager, they instantly fall in love with the book. Soon they have read all of Nesbit.

A few days later, their own magic begins. Jane spots a shiny round bit of metal in a crack in the sidewalk. She takes it to be a nickel, and puts it in her pocket. Later the same day, feeling a little bored, she wishes there'd be a fire. Within minutes the Toledo fires trucks go screaming by; the kids naturally follow. Eight blocks away, they find a rather elaborate child's playhouse crackling in flames. Apparently Jane got her wish, but on a small scale.

Two more events like this, and the children have worked out that what Jane found is truly a magic charm, but one that grants only half of what you ask. For example, Martha, the youngest child, only six, gets hold of the charm and wishes that Carrie, the family cat, could talk. "'Purrxx,' said Carrie the cat. 'Wah oo merglitz. Fitzahhh!'" Carrie is half-talking.

Carrie hates being compelled to talk, even in this garbled way, and demands to be returned to mewing. Jane has an idea. "I wish that Carrie the cat may in future say nothing but the word 'music,'" she says. She's thinking, of course, of the first syllable.

> "'Sick!' said Carrie the cat. 'Sick sick sick sick sick.'
> She *looked* sick."

This is the sort of thing that makes the book such a pleasure. The children always have to guess how the half magic will work. They get almost as clever as lawyers at wording things carefully, but they get tricked from time to time right to the end.

Meanwhile, they have spent a good while in King Arthur's England, a shorter time in a strange house in Toledo where Jane has by mistake turned herself half into someone else, and so on. It's a funny, charming, timeless book, as much pleasure to read to a child now as it was forty years ago. Those who got it read to them then may even have an obligation to pass on the pleasure now.

Lucy Boston wrote six books about Green Knowe and Edward Eager wrote seven that employ magic. Nearly all are worth reading, but in each case the first is the best. *The Children of Green Knowe* has a special claim in that it ranks with Dickens's *A Christmas Carol* and Rumer Godden's

Holly and Ivy as a perfect thing to read just before Christmas. But *Half Magic* is so joyous. Both books are all magic.

The Children of Green Knowe.
Lucy Boston. 1954.

Half Magic.
Edward Eager. 1954.

❧ *13* ❧

The Jailbird's Daughter

THE VERY FIRST THING the reader learns about Queenie Peavey is that she chews tobacco. (Don't go bringing the Surgeon General into this—the year is about 1935, and the place is rural Georgia. The teachers, etc., who disapprove of this thirteen-year-old girl biting into a plug of Brown Mule are not worried that it might be hazardous to her health. They just think it's unladylike.)

The second thing the reader learns about Queenie Peavey is that she is better than any other girl *or* boy in the eighth grade at throwing rocks. The third thing is that the local judge wants to see her.

Before the first chapter is over, the reader has watched Queenie, accompanied by two male friends, both twelve year olds, saunter over to the courtroom, where she is supposed to meet Judge Lewis. A trial is under way, and the three children sit down in the courtroom to wait. To pass the time, they each take a chew of Brown Mule. No sin in that: The courtroom is generously furnished with spittoons. But Queenie can't resist spitting at the woodstove instead—it makes a fine hiss and crackle when she hits. The judge is naturally furious.

The reader has also seen Queenie walking home, heard a town kid taunting her because her father is in jail, and watched her respond with two well-aimed stones. (She is throwing to scare, not to hit. This is a little kid.) And the reader has seen her bring down a squirrel sixty feet up in an oak tree with one perfectly aimed stone, greatly annoying a town lady who disapproves for the squirrel's sake, for the sake of Southern womanhood, and on several other grounds as well. Queenie, unperturbed, takes the dead squirrel on out to the run-down little farm where she and her mother live; it will be the centerpiece of their supper.

By now the reader may think he has encountered one of those well-known caricatures of rural Southern life, designed chiefly to give urban Southerners and Northerners of all kinds a pleasing sense of superiority. Al Capp's comic strip "L'il Abner" was like that, with a bit of sex thrown in.

The reader would be quite mistaken. *Queenie Peavey* is certainly a vivid book, and Queenie herself has a stronger personality than most, though not all, of the thirteen year olds I have known. But in no way is it caricature. On the contrary, the book seems to me a wonderfully sensitive and accurate evocation of the way children really deal with each other, and simultaneously a nice portrait of a small Southern high school sixty years ago. Nor is that all. At the heart of the book is the account of how an early adolescent successfully copes with the loss of an illusion that has been central to her life. (When Daddy gets home, everything will be all right.)

To sense the richness of the book, you need only go on to the second chapter. It's as quiet as the first chapter was rowdy. Queenie has now walked almost the whole mile and a half out from town to the two-room cabin where she and her mother live. Right now she is passing Elgin Corry's little farm—the Corrys are the only other people on the washed-out old road. They're a black family with a much better house than the Peaveys (it's brick, and Elgin built it), but otherwise they live on the same subsistence level.

Elgin has two children, an eight-year-old son named Dover and a five-year-old daughter named Avis. Both consider

Queenie a good friend. There's nothing in the least virtuous or let's-all-be-interracial-together about this. Those three are all the kids there are in the neighborhood, and in perfect unself-consciousness they spend a lot of time together. Dover and Queenie are particularly fond of telling improbable stories to Avis. At five, Avis is an imaginative but exceedingly gullible child. They are able to convince her that, for example, the old family dog is an expert tree climber, often to be seen at the tops of the taller pines.

This particular afternoon, Dover and Avis can only stay at Queenie's a little while; then Queenie is home alone. Her mother works long days for low pay at the local cannery, and by the time she has walked home from her job it is usually dark. So Queenie does the chores. Today that means she skins the squirrel, feeds the chickens, and splits the next day's stovewood. Then, in a charming kind of idyll, she pretends that Ol' Dominick the rooster is an appreciative audience asking her to sing, and she sings the old song "Foolish Questions" for him. It is no pretense but plain fact that Dominick is a pet. He is Queenie's chief company when Dover and Avis aren't around, and he is a good deal smarter (and more affectionate) than most city people ever dream a chicken can be. I have known one or two Vermont chickens like him.

By now it is getting dark. Queenie goes over to Elgin's barn where, by prearrangement, she milks their one cow. The Peavey cowshed collapsed some years back. Letting Queenie use his barn is not just charity on Elgin's part: In return he gets to graze his team of mules in the Peaveys' pasture when his own grass runs short. Worn out though it is, it still can handle more than a single cow.

The book more or less alternates this way, with Queenie being a troublemaker at school in town and a hard-working, hard-studying, lonesome child in the country. Then her father comes home on parole. There is an almost unbearably sad chapter as the excited Queenie tries to treat him as a loving father, and gets rebuff after rebuff. There is also a sharp realistic touch concerning the neighbors. As soon as Elgin Corry hears that Mr. Peavey is home, he forbids his children to go over to Queenie's any more. He's not being a snob about a convict, like some of the people in town. He's just well aware, though he never says it plainly, that Mr. Peavey might order them off the place, and call them some very unpleasant names as he did so.

The book ends—well, I guess I'm not going to say how it ends, since my aim is to tempt people to read it. But I virtually guarantee that you'll like the ending.

One warning: the book does have a quality that some people may regard as a fault. Certain of its characters get preachy from time to time. Myself, I don't consider that a fault. When the *author* does, yes. That's generally a fault, or at least a strategic error. Characters are another matter.

Jesus got preachy from time to time, too—and was rightly admired for it. There is good preaching and bad preaching. Good preaching is a wonderful thing, in real life, and, yes, in novels, too. In *Queenie Peavey* the sermon is on courage, and for a reader of almost any age, it is a stirring one to hear.

Queenie Peavey.
Robert Burch. 1966.

ᵈ§ *14* §ᵈ

Way Out West in Egypt Land

W HEN I WAS A BOY of twelve, I had two friends. With one of them I did real-world things. We would take the train into New York City (then a safe enough place for middle-class kids from the suburbs) and go to double-feature movies. We sailed in boats on the fringes of Long Island Sound.

With my other friend, though, I lived almost entirely in an imaginary world. Many afternoons a week we would come home from school and instantly take up our roles in a sort of medieval kingdom. Note the plural. He might be an enemy king at 4 P.M., the captain of our palace guard at 4:10, a rebel duke at 4:53, and (very reluctantly) a beautiful princess just before whichever of us had to go home had to leave. *Some* female roles were needed, and we played every-thing. Just once we tried admitting the boy who liked dou-ble features and sailboats. It was a dismal failure. He never even managed to perceive his broomstick as a lance.

One of the great divisions among children is between those who go on liking to play pretend games after the early years (*all* very small children play them) and those who by eight or ten see such games as foolishness.

I'm not claiming that one kind is better than the other, certainly not in the sense of pointing to a richer or happier life. Gordon, the boy who liked reality and scorned his broomstick lance, has been far more successful than either Jack or me. He has half a dozen enterprises, all thriving. We both became what the Japanese, putting in an r for an l, call *sararimen*—minor employees of large organizations.

But I do make the modest claim that it is well to know which kind of child you are dealing with before you drop into a bookstore to get the kid something for Christmas. And if the child happens to be a role-player, between the ages of about nine and fifteen, I do have a book to suggest. Get that child Zilpha Keatley Snyder's *The Egypt Game*.

There are tons of books about imaginary worlds. I love most of them. Most of the well-written ones, anyway. But in nearly all cases the imaginary world is entered either by magic (you walk right into a painting, you climb a bean-stalk, you drink a potion) or by science (you arrive in your starship). Either way, the world was already there, and it is merely a matter of reaching it. But in *The Egypt Game,* the world is not a pre-existing one. It is created by its charac-ters. Watching them do it is the very best part of the book. The first creator you meet is an eleven-year-old girl named April Hall. April has just arrived in northern California to spend what she erroneously supposes will be a few weeks with her grandmother. She didn't want to come. She has liked it just fine, living in Hollywood with her glamorous mother, a bit player in the movies. Grandma's only a librar-ian, at what seems to be the University of California at Berkeley. April is precociously bright, wears huge false eye-lashes, talks grown-up, and in general is sure to annoy any normal healthy child.

She doesn't annoy Melanie Ross, though. Melanie's a girl her own age whose family lives in the same small, shabby apartment house as April's grandmother. Melanie is a born role-player who has never happened to meet some-one like herself, and so has always gone alone into her imaginary worlds. She instantly recognizes April as another of her kind, and welcomes her, eyelashes and all.

By the fourth chapter the two girls are close friends. They play together every day. Just now they're talking a lot about Egypt—they're even going to the city library and reading up on the old Egyptian gods and rituals. At the end of the chapter they begin to create their world.

At a similar moment, God Himself used a starter kit. You'll remember that when He decided to create the human race, He didn't make the first person out of nothing. He took a big handful of dust, shaped it, breathed on it, and so fashioned Adam. There's something about a rib, too. If God Himself did that, certainly these two little girls needed props when they started to create the Land of Egypt.

What made it all possible was Melanie's discovery of a loose board in a fence surrounding a storage yard. The yard is behind a run-down antique shop, and in it are many suggestive things: a crumbling bust of Nefertiti, queen of Egypt; a lot of wooden columns from some dismantled house; a shed that almost demands conversion to a Temple of Sacrifice. Within minutes the game begins.

It rapidly develops over the next few weeks. April and Melanie use the bust of Nefertiti to decorate their first altar, which soon comes to belong to Isis, goddess of goodness and beauty. Next they are inspired (April particularly) to make an altar for Set, god of evil. They begin to make sacred fires in an old mixing bowl. They find the Crocodile Stone, and dedicate it to Set. Before many weeks, they almost begin to believe in the power of what they have evoked. Please note the "almost." There are no cheap Stephen King thrills in this book, with the bust of Nefertiti coming eerily to life, or the mixing bowl being haunted, or whatever. The thrills in *The Egypt Game* are more expensive, much more plausible, and mixed with a good deal of comedy. This book is funny, as well as highly imaginative.

But though Nefertiti doesn't come to life, the game itself does; and like any living thing, it keeps growing. In the

beginning there were just April and Melanie, plus Melanie's four-year-old brother Marshall, who she has to take
care of after school, because her mother is off teaching and
her father is a graduate student at the university. Marshall
is happy to be a boy pharaoh.

Then a new girl named Elizabeth Chung moves into the
apartment house, and turns out to have good Egypt potential. Chung, did I say? She's Chinese-American? Yes. Melanie and Marshall are black, for that matter, and a Japanese-
American boy will be along shortly. This is no virtue-book,
however, preaching ethnic tolerance. Human diversity is
something it takes casually for granted. It's entirely for her
own sake that Elizabeth gets admitted to the priesthood of
the Land of Egypt.

Somewhat later the three high priestesses and the boy
pharaoh are joined by two high priests. That is, on the night
of Halloween, two boys from their sixth-grade glass discover the fenced yard, and promptly invade. At first they
threaten to tell, but one of them in particular is fascinated
by the altars of Isis and Set, and by the rituals the girls have
devised. All this appeals to his own fertile mind. In the end,
Toby Alvillar and Ken Kamata join up.

Ken's role is rather like that of Gordon in my own childhood, but Toby is a full participant. He is the one who now
introduces all the Egyptians to the study of hieroglyphics,
and it is he who gets so carried away with the Oracle of
Thoth that all six Egyptians scare themselves half to death.

Wouldn't *you* be a little nervous, if you started leaving
written questions in the beak of a stuffed owl that you are
pretending is the god Thoth, and the owl starts giving written answers? Wouldn't you be even more nervous, if you
were Toby, and had been sneaking out at night to write the
answers, but the third night you couldn't get out and there
was an answer anyway? In a strange handwriting? Saying
something it would seem as if only a god could possibly
know? I think you might be.

Zilpha Snyder is justly famous for her ability to invent realistic and likeable child characters. All six of the main characters here are a pleasure to read about, including Ken, the all-American athlete. As for the game itself, it sounds wonderful. I wish Jack and I had been in the Land of Egypt, instead of our nameless and eventually rather boring medieval kingdom. If I wasn't afraid the sixth graders would laugh, I'd go now.

In fact, maybe I was wrong to say that this book is for one type of kid between the ages of nine and fifteen. Though grown-ups would read it differently, with reminiscent smiles, it may really be for one type of people, up to the age of a hundred or so.

The Egypt Game.
Zilpha Keatley Snyder. 1967.

~§ *15* ੨०

Dear Diary? Delightful Diary!

*S*ABRINA LIND is eleven years old. She and her eight-year-old brother James are the two children in an upper-class English family. They live in a big house called Thornfield, which is in a village also called Thornfield. The house is so old that an American can barely imagine it. It was already five hundred years old when Columbus discovered America.

Like many girls her age, Sabrina keeps a diary. Even if these were normal times, she would have a lot to write about. There are horses to ride at Thornfield, owls to hear in the woods, interesting characters in the village to talk to, important visitors from London.

But these are not normal times. The year is 1940, and Europe is at war. Poland is lost; France has fallen. Now Hitler is preparing to invade England. There is a rush to get as many children as possible away from what may soon be a battlefield. In their thousands, English children are shipped off to Canada and the U.S. The parents stay behind.

I Go by Sea, I Go by Land is a book consisting entirely of Sabrina's diary, starting on the day she and James learn they are to be sent to America. The first bomb has just fallen near their house, which is in Sussex, right on the invasion route. Their father tries to be cheerful, and tells them it's a great chance to see the world, and how when he was little he always wanted to be a cabin boy on a ship. Sabrina and James are not cheered, though they pretend to be. "We do not want to be cabin boys and see the world if there is a war on in England," Sabrina writes in her diary. "We want to stay here."

Less than a week later they are boarding a boat train that will take them to the port where they'll be put on a ship to Canada. The two parents stand helplessly on the platform as the train full of children and mothers with babies pulls out of the station. They will not see Sabrina and James again until the war is over; perhaps they will never see them again. The father has just been called up by the Royal Air Force; the mother must survive years of the blitz. James is weeping with his hands over his face; Sabrina is being brave. The train moves off.

Does this sound like a mournful diary? Well, it's not. It's one of the funniest, most charming diaries I ever saw. The darkness of the war is present—the ship they sail on has to go in a convoy, for example, and the danger of being torpedoed is so great that the convoy is escorted by three destroyers and a battleship. But it is only a backdrop of darkness. The foreground is bright and shining. James and Sabrina are both very imaginative children, and Sabrina is a born writer. Sometimes she is deliberately funny, and sometimes she is funny without meaning to be.

An example: One of the friends they make on the voyage is the ship's First Officer, whom Sabrina greatly admires. (Well she might. He is kind and wise and brave.) So when someone asks her the question adults are always asking kids—what is she going to be when she grows up—she has an answer ready. "I said I might be a First Officer or perhaps a Clown in the circus because I like both but perhaps I would rather have some children. About six boys, with one or two girls sprinkled in." That "sprinkled" is pure Sabrina. So is the shortage of punctuation. And no Zero Population Growth moralizing, please. Sabrina was writing in 1940. World population was a bit over 2 billion, not the present 5.8 billion.

But I am getting ahead of the story. Back to the train. The children are not totally bereft when it steams out of London. They know someone on board, who will also be on the ship with them. This is a woman called Pel, a close friend of their parents. Pel is young—in her early thirties— but already a famous writer. She is being evacuated because she has a six-month-old baby.

Pel is at least as imaginative as Sabrina and James, and by the time they board the ship she has them doing what their father failed to: treating the whole thing as an adventure. For example, back in 1940 it was normal to get seasick, except on the smoothest crossings. Effective nausea medicine had not yet been invented. On the second day of the voyage Sabrina notes in her diary that the ship has begun to pitch and roll, and the child passengers are getting sick. Does she complain? Point out that if she'd been allowed to stay at Thornfield, her stomach would be fine? No. For herself and James she is clinically observant, and for Pel she is full of admiration:

> I have been sick three times and James has been sick
> five times. Pel cannot afford to be sick because she
> has to look after Romulus and bath and feed him
> and wash the napkins because there are so few stew-
> ardesses. But still she is sick all the same.

Those napkins, of course, are what we call diapers.

Another friend they make on the voyage is a Cockney girl just Sabrina's age. She is one of three hundred working-class London children being evacuated on this ship, and she is dreadfully homesick. How do they meet?

This morning we were walking down a corridor
with Pel and we looked into a cabin and there was a
girl sitting on a bunk crying. Not sobbing, just big
tears running slowly down her face on to her hands.
. . . Pel, who can't bear to see anybody cry, went in
and asked her what was the matter and the girl said
she didn't know. "As Bad as That?" said Pel and the
girl nodded. . . . So we all cried a little which was
better than only one and Pel took us back to her
cabin and we had Eau de Colougne behind our ears
and sniffs of smelling salts which made us sneeze.
Pel said. "Well, it can't be helped. Let's forget all that
and have a pillow fight." So we did that and the electric light was broken and we felt relieved.

Well, by now you know how Sabrina writes, and I hope
you are itching to read more of her. There is lots more *to*
read. At this point their convoy of eight ships (plus the
three destroyers and the battleship) is only three days out.
There is all the rest of the voyage to come, and their days in
Canada, the flight to New York, and then their adventures,
great and small, during their first three months of living
with an American family in one of the grander New York
suburbs. Always the chief interest is how these two clever
children from an old house in the Old World respond to our
New World. I'll quote Sabrina just once more. She rather
likes the fast pace of American life:

One of the best things about America is that you do
not ever have to wait for anything. For instance, if
you want ice you have only to go and get it from the
Referigitator. We never had a Referigitator at home,
only blocks of ice that Mr Tanner, the United
Dairies, brings out every second day, except Sundays
when he hands round the Plate in Church.

II

One question remains. Sabrina is such a very good writer, even if she can't spell "refrigerator." Did an eleven-year-old girl really keep this marvelous diary, or are she and it the invention of some adult writer, the way Holden Caulfield is the invention of J. D. Salinger or Robinson Crusoe the invention of Defoe? Is the book fiction or nonfiction?

The answer is that it's both. It's fiction, all right. The diary was not written by an eleven-year-old girl but by a thirty-four-year-old woman. To be precise, it was written by Pel.

But it's also fact. As a character in the diary Pel is a famous writer, and in the real world Pel is also a famous writer. Only there her name is Pamela Lyndon Travers—P. L. Travers on the title pages of the Mary Poppins books. (The first one came out in 1934.) It is an easy jump from P. L. to Pel.

Furthermore, like Pel, P. L. crossed the Atlantic with a shipful of children in August 1940, and like her she spent the next two years in the U.S. Sabrina and James were with her, I believe, though not under those names.

But listen to P. L. herself. Here is what she wrote in 1940:

> The characters in Sabrina's diary and the experiences
> recorded are authentic. It is a personal record and
> certain names have necessarily been altered. Also, in
> view of conditions in Great Britain at the time of
> writing it seemed wiser to suppress specific dates
> and any mention of ports of sailing and to hide under
> the pseudonym of Thornfield the true identity of the
> village from which this journey started.

III

The book is not without flaws. There's a small one: P. L. gets a little carried away with humorous and improbable misspellings, such as having Sabrina nearly always write "dairy" when she means to refer to her diary. If the child is going to make that switch, shouldn't she make the corresponding one, and have Mr. Tanner work for United Diaries?

There is also a larger problem. Toward the end P. L. begins to hurry. Which means that Sabrina begins to skip. In a short entry on the last day of September she writes, "Life is so busy now that I cannot always keep up with my dairy." I guess not. Her first entry in October is one word long. Her second one is a single sentence. This becomes intensely frustrating for the reader, who has gotten used to hearing all the details and relishing every one of them.

Ms. Travers does slow down again for the final scene, which takes place on James's ninth birthday. Even if she didn't, *I Go by Sea* would still be a wonderful book—better than several of the Mary Poppinses, and as good as the best ones. I just wanted more.

I Go by Sea, I Go by Land.
P. L. Travers. 1941.

❧ *16* ❧

A Ten Year Old in Hollywood

NOEL STREATFEILD was one of those extraordinary writers who turn out books more or less the way a hen turns out eggs. The rebellious daughter of an English bishop, she ran away to become an actress. In her thirties, she began to write. Under her own name she wrote forty-five novels: some for grown-ups, some for kids. As Susan Scarlett, she wrote twelve more. Though she never touched nonfiction until she was nearing sixty, she then found time to produce seventeen books of nonfiction. Still, of course, writing frequent novels.

Usually a person who writes this much—two or three books every single year—is somewhat repetitious. Often such a person is slave to a formula. Noel Streatfeild was both. But not in every book. In her best books she approaches greatness.

Her closest approach comes in a series of children's books that I haven't mentioned yet: the so-called Shoes books. Called that because in the U.S. they all have the word "shoes" in the title: *Ballet Shoes, Theatre Shoes,* etc. All twelve are stories about artistically talented children, at least one of whom is usually a dancer. Eleven of them range from pretty good to very good; the twelfth is wonderful.

That book, of course, is *Movie Shoes.* It takes place in England and in California soon after World War II. England still has food rationing, bomb sites, austerity of every kind.

In London lives a family named Winter. The father is a writer, just now totally blocked and also sick. The mother is beautiful, artistic, kind, and ineffectual. Then there are three children. Rachel is twelve and a dancer. Tim is eight and a budding genius at the piano. Jane is ten, and likes dogs.

There's another difference as well. Rachel and Tim both have their mother's good looks. Jane isn't ugly, but there's absolutely nothing cute about her, in manner or appearance.

For the sake of Mr. Winter's health, this family is going to move to southern California for six months. Not being allowed to take more than a few pounds out of England, they are going to be guests of Mr. Winter's sister, who lives in Santa Monica. Aunt Cora married an American when she was eighteen, and has been in California ever since.

It is a measure of how different the world was fifty years ago that none of her relatives in England have seen Aunt Cora or even talked to her since her marriage. No one was jetting across the Atlantic in six hours; you sailed on the *Mauretania* and took a week. No one faxed or dialed from London to Santa Monica; only the rich used international phone service at all. The normal speed communication was an air-mail letter. Aunt Cora is going to be a major shock when they do meet her.

But even apart from aunts, the visit to California is not initially popular with the Winter kids. Rachel is going to lose her first professional opportunity—a chance to dance in a Christmas pantomime in London. Tim is going to lose a chance to get free lessons from a concert pianist. Jane is going to be forcibly separated from her dog.

The pleasure of the book is in seeing how this polite, talented (except for Jane) war-starved English family responds to lush, orange-juiced California—and how it responds to them. The most fun of all is their encounter with the movie business.

Jane is the one who makes contact. About their second day in California, she is walking along the beach, and sees a spaniel down at the waterline, eating a decomposed fish. Difficult with people, Jane is fierce and protective about animals. Soon she has figured out which house the spaniel came from, and is on the back porch giving its surprised owner a lecture in her small, elegant English voice. "Some people don't deserve to have dogs," she begins.

The spaniel's owner happens to be a young director for Bee Bee Studios. He is struck both with Jane's voice and with her scowl. Several weeks later he winds up giving her first a screen test, and then a part in his current film. This is not because she suddenly develops talent, or gets nice, or pretty, but because the part is for just such a sulky child as she, with just such an accent. He's filming *The Secret Garden.* The child star who was to play Mary has gotten sick; he takes Jane as an emergency replacement. The initial effect on her character is to make her even worse than before; along with everything else, she is now puffed up.

Movie Shoes is actually a kind of realistic fairy tale. It could even be called a modern variant on "Cinderella," this time with believable psychology. The original Cinderella is mistreated for years by her stepmother and stepsisters. As all who know the story will recall, this does not embitter her one bit. After her fairy godmother sets her up with good clothes, and she marries the Prince, her first act is to find noble and wealthy husbands for those same two stepsisters. That shows what a really nice person she is. (Unless, of course, you look at it from the point of view of the two husbands. Then you might wonder what kind of future *they* face.)

Jane is a good deal more probable. She's a Cinderella, all right, but through DNA, not just wicked stepmothers. She has a fairy godfather in Mr. Browne, the director—only his motive is to save his picture, and he is often, and justly, furious with Jane. She does not turn all oozy-sweet once she gets some recognition. On the contrary, her relations with Maurice Tuesday, her fellow child star in *The Secret Garden,* begin badly and get worse. He, being a real actor, is able to whisper spiteful things in the hope of upsetting her, and then half a second later look with big candid eyes at the camera, and tug at all hearts. She would probably kill him if she could. The interplay between these two is one of the funniest things in a book with many funny things.

I need to pause a second on the humor, because it's of a rare kind. Usually a child's book is funny in one of two ways. It's funny to the child, but seems a bit simpleminded to the adult reading aloud, who gets pleasure only vicariously, from the giggles and shining eyes of the child. Or it's funny for the grown-up, with secret adult touches, and half-wasted on the child, over whose patronized head the humor mostly goes.

Not in *Movie Shoes.* The enmity between Maurice and Jane is funny in a complex way to adults and in a direct and simple way to children. Ditto the highly unself-conscious behavior of Tim, the eight-year-old piano prodigy. Children laugh with pleasure because he talks in such a confident, slightly bookish way, and keeps saying startling things to grown-ups. Grown-ups are apt to be sorry he's only in a book, because they'd like to snatch him out and adopt him.

But good as the humor is, it's still not the best thing about the book. The best is its tremendous sense of motivation on the part of totally believable characters. Rachel is focused. Tim has two or three different focuses, among which he shifts with ease. Jane is a one-girl animal protection society. For children who lack a sense of direction, getting to know the Winter kids is something like being magnetized if you are an iron filing. And for parents, it's an irresistible encounter between two wildly different cultures.

Movie Shoes.
Noel Streatfeild. 1949.

❧ 17 ❧

The Kids Fight Back

*I*F THERE'S ONE experience all children have in common, it's that of being pushed around by much larger beings called adults. Even the most loving mother's arm, propelling a three-year-old the last ten feet across the street and onto the safe sidewalk—even that protective push reminds the child how much stronger these adults are. They can always win by force. If they didn't love you, you'd be in real trouble.

Many a child promises itself that it will never forget (as its parents so clearly have) what it feels like to be a kid in an adult-run world. In the turmoil of adolescence and the later thrill of gaining adult power, many an ex-child forgets feeling and promise both.

A few don't, however. Those few include most of the ones who grow up to be writers for children. Hence one of the dominant themes in children's literature: the struggle of the small-powerless-and-clever (or sometimes just the small-powerless-and-lucky) against the big and strong. Often enough it's presented directly and plainly as children vs. adults. But it also appears in a thousand disguised versions. There's Jack the Giant-Killer, for example, where the bad adult is put into another species, and hence Jack can get rid of him with no guilt. Or both sides become animals. Small creatures like rabbits and mice outwit the foxes and the cats. In a more complicated displacement, there are the many myths of "little people": brownies, elves, Tolkien's hobbits, and so on.

Then there is Jean Merrill's version in *The Pushcart War*. This semi-recognized classic is one of the funniest and most satisfying triumphs of small-and-clever I know. It can be read in four different ways, and they are all funny.

The book pretends to be the history of a war fought in New York City in the spring of 1986. Mrs. Merrill pretends she is recording that history ten years later, in 1996. Actually, she made the whole thing up, back during the time of the real war in Vietnam, to which there are some interesting parallels.

Her war begins as modern wars generally do: unannounced. A big country feels cross with a little country, which is doing something the big country doesn't want it to. The big country decides to intervene. But it does not declare war, as we did not in Vietnam and the Russians did not in Afghanistan. Instead it just starts intervening, generally with tragic results.

In Mrs. Merrill's comic variation, trucks are the equivalents of Great Powers (or adults), and pushcarts are the equivalents of small countries (or children). What the pushcarts are doing that is bad is taking up space on the streets.

Before the book begins, the owners of the three biggest trucking companies in New York have met in secret to discuss the traffic problem. They decide that the best solution is to force everything off the streets except their own giant trucks. They will eliminate pushcarts, private cars, and taxis, in that order. After that, they may wipe out small trucks. How will they do all this? In part by dirty politics, in part by intimidation, when necessary by force. Why pushcarts first? Because they are the smallest and safest target.

The war begins in the spring of 1986, as trucks begin deliberately nudging pushcarts out of their way. In the first

week alone they damage over a hundred, injuring an occasional peddler also. There is, of course, zero damage to
trucks.

Then on March 15 the war escalates. A particularly hard-
nosed trucker named Albert P. Mack rams hard into the
pushcart of a peddler known as Morris the Florist, who is
selling daffodils on West 17th Street. (Morris had refused to
vacate his space when Mack told him to.) The cart is destroyed, and old Morris is sent flying through the air to land
head-first in a barrel of pickles.

That finally rouses the peddlers. The very next day a
small crowd of them meets at the shop of Maxie Hammer-
man, the famous pushcart repairman. They decide to fight
back—but not with firebombs or poison gas or anything
like that. Instead they opt for a weapon of childlike simplic-
ity. It was in fact invented by a child, the young son of a
Spanish-speaking pushcart owner named Carlos, a dealer
in used cardboard. This little boy discovered that if you
stick a pin through a dried pea, and then grab your pea-
shooter, you can fire a shot that will puncture a balloon.
Why not a truck tire?

The counter-attack now begins, and it consists entirely
of peddlers blowing pea-pins into the rear tires of trucks.
After a very nice peddler named Frank the Flower is
caught and jailed, and becomes a popular hero, the war
widens. The children of New York join in. Truckers become
afraid even to drive down a block where there are a couple
of kids playing, so they speed up. Then they get stopped,
and while the cop is writing out the ticket, some eight year
old gets a tire. In the end, the trucking companies capitu-
late, and the historic agreement is signed that severely lim-
its the size of trucks in New York City.

I said the book was funny in each of four interpretations.
The first, of course, is as a literal story about trucks. Who,
except the U.S. Department of Transportation, doesn't
know that trucks have gotten too big? Too big for the roads,

that is. I once saw an estimate that on certain types of pave-
ment one of those giant tandem trucks, fully loaded, produces as much road wear as one hundred thousand cars.
Too big for other traffic, too. They are a menace to small ve-
hicles, which is all the rest of us. Plus they block city
streets. In real life there has been no historic agreement;
there has been worsening gridlock. "Trucks larger than the
state of Delaware blocking every intersection"—so begins
an account in *The New Yorker* of a trip across Manhattan
last summer. So a fantasy in which trucks are brought
under control is deeply satisfying.

Under this story is a fable about global politics. Mrs.
Merrill isn't blatant about it, any more than Swift was about
his underlying fable in *Gulliver's Travels,* but it's there. The
three big trucking companies are called the Three—and
Mrs. Merrill casually mentions that they were originally
called The Big Three,

> but this caused some confusion as the leaders of
> three important nations of the time were also called
> The Big Three, and after a city newspaper ran a
> headline announcing BIG THREE CARVE UP CHINA
> (over a story about Mammoth, LEMA, and Tiger
> Trucking buying out the China Carting & Storage
> Co.), there was some international trouble in the
> course of which Moscow was bombed by an Indo-
> Chinese pilot. After that the city papers referred to
> the three big trucking companies simply as The
> Three.

As I've suggested, the book is also about the adult world
as seen from a child's point of view, including a child's
cheerful disregard of probabilities. (Would a pea-pin really
puncture a truck tire? I made up a supply this fall, and fired
ten shots at one of the big rear tires of my farm tractor. Got
nowhere.) Such child-imagined scenes, as the one where

the mayor of New York sits down to his weekly poker game with The Three, are wonderful.

But maybe best of all, there is what I can only call a feminine reversal of masculine logic in this book. Mrs. Merrill mocks that logic when she puts the movie star Wenda Gambling on a TV program with three traffic experts (all male, all pompous). She gently teases it through the so-called Portlette Papers—the shorthand notes taken by a youthful cleaning woman (and shorthand student) named Miriam Portlette, who happened to overhear part of a secret late-night meeting of The Three. She turns male logic upside down with General Anna of the pushcart army. It is all delicious.

I say this well aware that some feminists will be outraged: I'm probably wrong about what I take to be feminine, and even if I'm right, I as a man have no right to say it. To them I would answer: read the book. You'll not only see I am right, you'll want to pat me on the head for (one passage excepted) liking it so much.

What's the passage? Well, when you get the book, look in chapter 4. You'll spot it at once.

The Pushcart War.
Jean Merrill. 1964.

A Tale of Two Brothers

O NCE UPON A TIME there were two brothers
named Alfred and Laurence. Alfred, the older
brother, was a great scholar, and had many pupils.
But Laurence, the younger brother, was an artist and worked
alone. He drew, he painted, he did illustrations for books
and magazines.

On the side, both brothers also wrote poetry. Alfred
wrote his secretly, and showed it to no one. But Laurence
began to publish his poems, first one book of them and
then another, until he had seven. He found writing books
such a pleasure that he almost stopped painting, and just
wrote—not only poetry but also novels, plays, essays, and
one more kind of writing that I will not tell you about yet.
For many years he was the famous brother.

Then, in 1896, when he was nearly forty, Alfred finally
published *his* first book of poems, paying the costs of publication himself. The book did not make a big splash. In
the first year it sold only 382 copies. Laurence was still the
famous brother, and he stayed so a good while longer. For
example, when the eleventh edition of the Encyclopedia
Britannica came out in 1910, Laurence got an entry all to
himself. Alfred got three lines tacked on the end of his
brother's entry. If you judge by quantity, that was just right.

By now Laurence had produced twenty-three books, and Alfred still had only the one.

But Laurence was about to be eclipsed. The brothers' last name was Housman, and Alfred was commonly known as A. E. His one book (at that time) is called *A Shropshire Lad*. By 1910 it was selling thousands of copies a year; soon it would sell tens of thousands. It is still selling now. A. E. Housman is probably not quite a great poet—his range is too narrow—but he is one of the two or three best minor poets in our language. Poor Laurence, though he went on to publish a total of sixty-five books (A. E. published a total of two), is barely a name now. No one reads his poetry or his novels, and only a fortunate handful know to enjoy his wonderful and rather odd plays. But his fairy tales are another matter. They, or the best of them, are probably immortal. Never again will Laurence be more famous than A. E., but neither is he doomed to extinction.

One doesn't think of fairy tales as having authors, not even if one has read every word of Hans Christian Andersen. Partly because of its traditional form, a fairy tale seems always to have been there, as if people had been telling it at least since the Middle Ages, and maybe since the Stone Age. Maybe no one wrote it down until Perrault came along in the seventeenth century, or the brothers Grimm at the beginning of the nineteenth, but it was there. What's more, many fairy tales really *are* both ancient and anonymous.

Many others, however, are not. Fairy tales have been written in every place and age, and they continue to be now. Shakespeare wrote one. A Victorian nobleman named Lord Brabourne wrote one called "The Princess with the Pea-Green Nose." About the middle of the nineteenth century, the Scottish author George MacDonald wrote one I specially love called "The Light Princess." About twenty years ago Sylvia Townsend Warner wrote a series of enchanting ones for *The New Yorker*. (These appeal much more to grown-ups than to children.)

A particularly rich crop of new fairy tales appeared in England in the last two decades of the nineteenth century and the first decade of the twentieth. Most of the best ones were by one person: Laurence Housman.

Take the one I consider the very best of all. It's called simply "A Chinese Fairy Tale." The hero is a small boy named Tiki-pu. He is an orphan.

Tiki-pu is currently more or less the slave of a painter whose name we never learn, an avaricious man who runs an art school with many students. It is Tiki-pu's job to sweep the studio, wash the students' paint brushes, run errands, stretch the rice paper. He gets many kicks, little food, no thanks.

Tiki-pu has just two comforts in his life. One is that occasionally a lazy student will have Tiki-pu grind his colors for him. A true artist, the little boy loves making the colors; sometimes, with a particularly rich purple, "his heart beat so that he gasped for joy."

His other comfort is to look at a painting that hangs at the far end of the studio. Most of the paintings on the walls are by the students or the only moderately skilled teacher, but the school is very old, and a few are by great painters who worked there long ago. The greatest painter of all is a man named Wio-wani "who had lived and passed from their midst more than three hundred years ago." (Note the ambiguous phrasing here. Housman doesn't quite say he died.) The painting at the far end is by Wio-Wani, and there is a story that goes with it. What it shows is a garden full of trees and sunlight—and, down a long path, a palace. This palace, says Wio-wani, now an old man, is where he would like to rest.

The painting is so masterly that the Emperor of that period hears about it and comes to see it. He is so attracted that he says he, too, would like to rest in that beautiful palace. And then Wio-wani steps into the painting, walks down the path, opens a low door in the palace wall, and turns and beckons to the Emperor: "But the Emperor did not follow, so Wio-wani went in by himself and shut the door between himself and the world forever."

Unlike the avaricious teacher or the careless pupils, Tiki-pu spends his nights in the studio, sleeping on the floor. This child is also the unpaid night watchman. He'd rather be a painter. Maybe he can teach himself, he thinks, and using stolen bits of paper and colors, and scraps of candle ends to see by, every night he tries. But he is only a young boy; he needs a teacher. And presently he thinks of Wio-wani. He will copy him.

The next night he sits down in front of the great painting, and tries to reproduce it. He cannot. It is too hard. But as he is crying (remember how young he is) the palace door in Wio-wani's own painting opens, and an old man comes down the path.

What happens next I am not going to say, because I hope to make readers so curious that they will want to go read the whole story for themselves.

What I'm going to do instead is mention that this story is not Housman's own favorite; he prefers a tale called "The Rain Child." The hero again is a small boy, the son of a deposed rajah. The new rajah, the usurper who killed his father, doesn't dare kill *him,* precisely because he is a rain child. If he dies an unnatural death, the drought that ended when he was born will return. But the new rajah has many ideas for leading the boy to a natural death, and meanwhile he ensures that no one will be kind to the boy. You may be sure that in the end the usurper outwits himself. And Housman is right; the story is wonderful.

Housman is also right, I think, when he calls "The Man Who Did Not Pray" the best story in any genre that he ever wrote; I'll just add that it comes so close to being a fairy tale, or at least it could be the thousand and second of the

Arabian nights, that anyone who likes them is pretty sure to like it. But like Sylvia Townsend Warner, it is perhaps more for grown-ups than for children.

Brother Laurence doesn't get written about much these days. (Brother Alfred does constantly.) So before I stop I want to bring up one work more. This is one of his many plays. It's called *Possession,* and it takes place in heaven. The scene bears no relation to clouds, pearly gates, etc., nor do the people have wings or wear robes.

What you see on stage is an upper-middle-class drawing room of the Victorian era. In it are a middle-aged maidservant and her elderly mistress. This is Miss Julia Robinson, who has been dead for seven years. She was allowed to choose where in heaven she would live, and she chose the heavenly version of her parents' house in London. Neither parent lives in it, though both are in heaven, and both make rather dramatic appearances. (You may not have wings in heaven, but you can "appear" at will; you can also vanish at will.)

The day of the play is the day Julia's sister Laura has died, and *she* soon turns up. And only a few hours later the third and mildest sister, Martha, arrives. She was killed in a train wreck on the way to Laura's funeral.

The rest of the play—it's one act—is conversation and in-fighting among the three sisters. What I like most about it is the conflict between two social codes: first the hypocritical, prudish, stately gentility of Victorian ladies, and second the clear-eyed honesty of the dead. Julia, as the longest dead, has the most of this; Laura, who is a truly horrible woman, has the least. She is a character one loves to hate; one even longs to enter the scene as Wio-wani entered the painting, and shake her till her teeth rattle.

Some time when you're thinking about your own reading pleasure, not a child's, see if your library has that one of Housman's sixty-five books called *The Golden Sovereign.* Check it out and read "Possession." Now go into the children's section and get *The Rat-Catcher's Daughter*, which contains "A Chinese Fairy Tale" and eleven of Housman's other fairy stories. You'll be glad you did. And you'll realize what a talented man Brother Laurence was.

The Rat-Catcher's Daughter (an American selection of stories first published between 1894 and 1905), 1974.
The Golden Sovereign (contains "Possession"), 1937.
Laurence Housman.

Tales at Tea-Time.
Lord Brabourne. (Edward Hugessen Knatchbull), 1872.

The Kingdoms of Elfin.
Sylvia Townsend Warner. 1977.

❧ *19* ❧

Many Tales of Three Brothers

I

SIR GEORGE DASENT was a much-traveled man. He was born on the West Indian island of St. Vincent in 1817; his ancestors had been living there and on Antigua for a hundred years. He went to school and then to college in England, shuttling back and forth for vacations by square-rigged ship.

When he graduated from Oxford he did not return to his tropical island. Instead he went on north, to an even colder place than England, up to Sweden, where he had been appointed secretary to the British ambassador. That was in 1840. Dasent almost instantly fell in love with Scandanavian folklore and Scandanavian literature, which in early days were much the same thing. Soon, having learned Icelandic, he began to translate the old epic poems: the Saga of Burnt Njal, of Gisli the Outlaw, and so on. He helped to edit an Icelandic-English dictionary. And with warm encouragement from Jakob Grimm (he of Grimm's fairy tales), Dasent began to read all the Swedish, Danish, and Norwegian fairy tales he could get his hands on. He was especially taken with the Norse tales that had recently been collected by Peter Christen Asbjornsen. In 1859 he published a thick volume of them, brilliantly translated.

And in 1862 he published a smaller *Selection of the Norse Tales, for the Use of Children.*

It was a truly magical book, except for the drab title. And that eventually got changed. The book had dozens of editions in the last quarter of the nineteenth century and the first half of the twentieth. Once or twice it appeared as *Norse Wonder Tales,* which is not much of an improvement. Then in 1912 it took on its present name: *East o' the Sun and West o' the Moon.* This is surely one of the great resonating titles of fairy-tale literature, like Lord Dunsany's *The King of Elfland's Daughter* or George MacDonald's *At the Back of the North Wind.*

Like most folk tales, those of Scandanavia are highly formulaic. Most of the formulas involve three of something, though sometimes it can be seven somethings or even twelve. There are three wishes one is granted, three giants of increasing size and power with whom one must do battle, three feathers that must be plucked from the dragon's tail. (You didn't know dragons had tail feathers? You clearly haven't read Scandanavian folk tales.)

Most of all, there are likely to be three sisters or three brothers as central characters. The youngest sister or brother is nearly certain to be the good person, as in *King Lear,* as in "Cinderella," as in almost half the thirty tales in *East o' the Sun.* In the case of brothers, there is a curious piece of nomenclature. The youngest one, the one who is probably going to get the princess and half the kingdom, is generally called Boots. He is in Dasent, anyway.

That puzzled me when I was a little boy, demanding over and over that my father read these stories to me. Why Boots? It didn't seem to have anything to do with Puss in Boots or the seven-league boots. It did seem an odd thing to call someone who often had a perfectly good real name, like John or Peter. Not that I spent a lot of time worrying about it. As a youngest child myself, I mainly just waited for my character in the story to win.

When I was a few years older, and reading *East o' the Sun* to myself, I had gained enough linguistic sophistication to know that in England people who shined shoes were called bootblacks, and that in very large households the person who had to deal with all that footwear was some-times just called Boots. Even as the person in charge of the kitchen was sometimes just called Cook. It still seemed a peculiar name for the youngest of three wealthy brothers, let alone the most recently born of three princes. Only much later did I learn that Boots was also slang of Dasent's time for the junior officer in a regiment (who certainly did *not* black the colonel's boots) or the newest member of a posh club.

II

There are several remarkable things about Norse fairy tales, at least as translated by Dasent. One is a complete absence of prudery. Common sense is the prevailing ethic, common sense as applied in a magical world.

Take the story called "The Old Dame and Her Hen." The old dame is a widow with three daughters who owns one solitary chicken. She is that poor. One day the hen ventures too far from the widow's little cottage, falls through a trapdoor, and so becomes the property of the troll who lives under the hill. The widow sends her eldest daughter to look for it, and *she* falls through the trapdoor.

"Will you be my sweetheart?" asks the troll, who is wait-ing inside, and the girl says no, she has to find the hen. This so infuriates the troll that he rips her head off. It's the same with the second daughter. Not that I entirely blame the girl for refusing. This is an exceptionally ugly troll, and it's not as if he's offering marriage or anything.

The youngest daughter handles things much better. When she falls through the trapdoor and is propositioned by the troll, she spots the bodies in the cellar and answers, "With all my heart." They begin to live together that night.

Don't think this is fun. There is no silly sentimentality about his really being a decent sort when you get to know him. He is a troll who rips people's heads off, and she never forgets it. In the end she outsmarts him. She is able to bring her sisters back to life, to get her hands on nearly his whole hoard of gold and silver, and finally to cause him to stay out too late one night and get destroyed by the first rays of the sun. If it troubles her to have lost her virtue to such a monster, the story doesn't mention it.

She's only a peasant girl, to be sure; perhaps her virtue isn't worth much. But the same sensible attitude is taken by nearly all the princesses in the book. There's a princess imprisoned by the Dragon of Deepferry, for example—the same that had three feathers in his tail. She's been living with the dragon for years—not because she likes him, but because the alternative would be instant annihilation.

Princesses who are living safely at home in their fathers' palaces also tend to be accessible. *East o' the Sun* contains several variants of a plot that goes like this. Some third son—maybe a prince in disguise, maybe just an ordinary youth—has gotten hold of three objects made of pure gold. This youth—let's call him Boots—sits outside the palace, perhaps idly tossing a gold comb in the air. The princess sees him out the window, and she wants that comb. Boots won't sell it. But he'll freely give it to her in return for the chance to sleep one night on the floor of her bedroom. Usually right by the door, that first night, but remember: Boots has two more gold objects to tempt her with. On succeeding nights he gradually works closer. Only in a story Dasent omitted from the children's edition does he actually make it under the covers (the princess gets pregnant, and her father throws her out of the palace), but all the princesses will bargain at least a little.

Another striking thing about Norse fairy tales is the mixture of Christianity and paganism. One is laid on top of the other, like that Italian church called Santa Maria Sopra Minerva (St. Mary on top of the goddess Minerva). In their original form, some of the tales had gods in them as well as trolls. Odin and Loki would come down to walk about the earth.

That wouldn't do, of course, after Christianity came, and yet the stories were too good just to drop. So an occasional tale will begin, "Once on a time in the days when our Lord and St. Peter used to wander on earth . . ." And then you find Jesus giving someone three wishes, or getting annoyed with a stingy old woman and turning her into a woodpecker. Utterly unlike himself in the New Testament, but very like Odin.

This particular charm is wasted on small children, but the third one I'm going to mention is not. Nearly all fairy tales—nearly all old ones, anyway—were told, not written. They had the strength of the vernacular; they had immediacy, and a kind of childlike freshness. But later, when they got written down, many of them lost some of that freshness, because they got polished up and made more literary.

This did not happen with Dasent. Nothing of the nineteenth century and nothing of the Oxford scholar appears in his versions. You could easily take him for a contemporary of Gisli and Njal. The childlike freshness is still there, and children love it.

Since the subject is fairy tales, perhaps I should stop at three. But I shan't. I want to bring up one more charm. The Norse tales are indeed formulaic, but the old tellers felt quite free to play with the formula. The customary ending, for example, in cases where the story concludes with a marriage, is that the wedding feast lasts nine days and then the young couple live happily ever after. The Norse tales say nothing about happily ever after, and they play endless variations with the feast. When the Princess gets married in "The Glass Hill," her father outdoes himself with the

reception. "All I can say is," the story ends, "if they haven't
left off their merry-making yet, why they're still at it." In
"The Seven Foals," the hitherto invisible teller of the tale
attends the feast. "I was there, too," he says,

> but there was no one to care for poor me; and so I
> got nothing but a bit of bread and butter, and I laid it
> down on the stove, and the bread was burnt and the
> butter ran, and so I didn't get even the smallest
> crumb. Wasn't that a great shame?

For us readers, though, there's a whole smorgasbord.

> *East o' the Sun and West o' the Moon.*
> George W. Dasent. 1862.

∞ 20 ∞

It Is Permitted to Try Again

ANNE LINDBERGH is the novelist of second chances. During her brief lifetime she wrote a dozen fantasy novels for children, and about ten of them offer second chances to one or more characters.

All Americans believe in second chances, of course—it's one of our national characteristics, and to me a very appealing one. What's more, our society really does offer them: people going back to college at thirty-five or even eighty-five; people finding happiness in a second or even a third marriage; people shifting jobs in midcareer. But Lindbergh's second chances are something special.

The extreme case occurs in a novel called *The Shadow on the Dial*. Two children have been parked with their Uncle Doo (actually a great-uncle) while their parents enjoy a well-earned week of freedom on the Florida keys.

Uncle Doo turns out to be a sour old man of eighty, who has enjoyed very little of his life. He never developed the musical promise he showed as a boy, never had a job he really cared about, never married, never even learned to cook a decent meal. At eighty he has become so negative that the kids privately call him Uncle Don't.

Remember that the book is fantasy—a fantasy written for children between ten and fourteen. When the two children in the book find that Uncle Doo as a boy almost inherited a really good flute, and they also discover that while in Florida they can do a limited amount of time-traveling, they get a bright idea. Maybe all he needed was a jump start. They decide to go back and rearrange events in 1915 so that he *will* inherit the flute. At some risk they do. The flute becomes his. But nothing else changes at all. When they come back to 1985 and Uncle Doo's crummy little Florida condo, they are greeted by the same sour old man.

These kids don't give up easily. They return to Uncle Doo's childhood and young manhood five different times, in each case making one change. The fifth one finally works. And how! When they get back this time, not only is there a vigorous and cheerful old man in the apartment, a retired flutist with the Boston Symphony, but also a woman who they had met back in their time travels and liked a lot. Only now she has been married to Uncle Doo for forty-three years. This is a lovely book.

It's not Anne Lindbergh's best, though. Her best is called *Nick of Time*. Some people, I admit, would claim that honor for *The People of Pineapple Place* (which I would place second). But whoa! Before I say another word about her books, I need to say a few about the author herself— about who she isn't and who she is.

Who she isn't is her mother. Her mother, Anne Morrow Lindbergh, wrote *Gift From the Sea* and a good many other books, but no fantasy novels. People naturally enough get those confused; *Books in Print* somewhat less naturally does. You cannot trust the entry for either.

Who she is, or rather was, was her own woman. But she was also my wife. It was a third chance for us both, and from the start so successful that we decided to regard our previous matrimonial ventures as training marriages. So how can you trust me, who was her loving and delighted husband, any more than you can trust *Books in Print*? Answer: Because I knew her writing before I knew her, indeed had read two of her books aloud to children. At the time I formed my high opinion, I had no idea that their author was something pretty close to an ideal wife.

But back to *Nick of Time*. It takes place entirely in the town of Alcott, New Hampshire. There are twelve major characters, most of them either thirteen or nine years old, and all but one of them connected with a tiny private school called Mending Wall. It has eight students and three teachers, and it is totally progressive, caring, sensitive, environmental, and, to the locals, weird. The students include Jericho, the thirteen-year-old boy who narrates the story (and who has the liveliest of styles); his poetry-mad roommate BVD; Alison, the thirteen-year-old girl Jericho is in love with; and Bunny, a wonderfully lovable thirteen-year-old feminist. Also Maple, a nine-year-old student who once, out of pure loyalty to her brother, eats a cockroach.

Lindbergh makes the school a place of high comedy. Mending Wall's annual soccer match with a local public school (which always has to lend them two or three players just to fill out the team)—that match alone is worth the price of the book. The scene where Maple eats the cockroach is even better.

But you don't wind up laughing at the school. On the contrary, you probably wind up wishing you'd gone there, or that you could send your children there. Mending Wall is in fact based on a slightly larger progressive school in Vermont where Lindbergh taught for two years while her son was a student there. She loved the place, just also saw its comic side. The real school, incidentally, I believe to be the only grades 5–8 institution in the United States that regularly builds electric cars and enters them in races. One of the teachers has to drive, of course, since none of the students is old enough to have a license, but the whole school comes along for the race.

I said all but one of the major characters is connected with Mending Wall. That one is Nick, the title character. Nick lives in the very same building that houses the little school, but he lives there a hundred years later, in 2094. By now the small town of Alcott has become the large and rather boring city of Glen Alcott, and the long-defunct school is a museum, with numerous exhibits of late-twentieth-century life. Nick's parents curate it.

Nick manages to time-travel back to Mending Wall in 1994, and then Jericho, Alison, and Bunny manage to time-travel forward and visit him in 2094. Here I think Lindbergh shows actual genius. Most predictions of the future are kind of flat-footed, and this is true whether it's a happy future or one disaster after another. But as Jericho, Alison, and Bunny take in the future with their very bright thirteen-year-old minds, it's more like dancing. Lindbergh is even funnier about 2094 than she is about the school, but she's also perfectly serious, both in what she likes about the future and what dismays her.

Ah, but what about second chances? Don't worry. Though the United States is painfully overcrowded in 2094—the city of Glen Alcott butts right up to the adjoining and equally boring city of Alcott Heights—we are *still* the land of second chances. Alison gets one.

At the time of the book Alison is about to be withdrawn from Mending Wall, much against her will. Alison's mother is not progressive, sensitive, or environmental. She's not even a good mother. She more or less dumped Alison at Mending Wall five years ago when she moved away from Alcott in order to help run a chain of teen beauty shops, all called Curly Girl. Alison has now grown into a pretty girl, and her mother intends to use her in the business. Never mind that Alison despises everything Curly Girl stands for, prefers jeans, a sweatshirt, and no makeup. Her mother has every intention of re-dressing her in color-coordinated outfits of various sickening hues, slathering her face with stuff and goo, perming her hair, and then featuring her in Curly Girl TV ads.

As the mother perceives life, this is doing Alison a big

favor. As Alison and everyone else at Mending Wall perceive it, this is cruel and unnatural punishment. What happens? Alison gets a second chance—at parents, that is.

She has met a really nice couple in 2094 who are excellent parents. That's no surprise, because in this particular
future you have to pass an exam before you can get married,
and a much bigger one before you can start a family. Her
couple have a son, have always wanted a daughter. Alison
successfully migrates to the future, from which no missing
persons search is going to bring her back kicking and
screaming to Curly Girl. Jericho is desolated, of course. But
I told you Bunny was lovable. She is also quite capable of
taking the initiative. Jericho gets a second chance, too.

There are many other delights in the book, such as the
seventy or so wisecracking footnotes that Jericho can't resist putting in the book. Such as the whole complex, ideal-
istic personality of Jericho's father, who is the headmaster
(he doesn't call it that) of Mending Wall. Such as all the in-
genious ways Lindbergh plays off lines of Robert Frost.

But I've said enough. You've got your chance to pick up
Nick of Time. It's in print, and in many libraries. This being
the real world, you may not get a second chance. You may
forget, or, painful thought, the book may one day go out of
print. Better grab it now.

Nick of Time.
Anne Lindbergh. 1994.

◆§ *21* §◆

An Adventure a Day

*J*OYCE CAROL OATES, Noel Streatfeild, and Laurence Housman are not the only prolific writers in the world. There is also E. Nesbit.

Edith Nesbit, an Englishwoman who was born in 1858 and lived until 1924, averaged better than two books a year throughout her adult life. Forty novels for children! Nine for adults. Five books of verse for children. Twenty-two books of poetry for adults. Plays, essays, a book about royal children—real ones, like the two princes in the Tower of London. In her spare time she edited still more books, such as a child's Shakespeare.

Don't, however, imagine her holed up in a garret. She was a profoundly social creature, one of the founders of the Fabian Society, and hence of the Labor Party in England. She had two husbands (one at a time), three children, and for many years a household situation such as you might not dream could have existed in Victorian England. Wanda Gág is not the only bohemian here. There is also E. Nesbit.

The wonder is that with all this going on, so many of her books are so good. I don't claim they all are. You won't miss much if you fail to read her early collection of stories called *Pussy and Doggy Tales*. But you do miss considerable if you go through childhood and then parenthood or godparenthood without reading any of her books about the sand fairy and the five children. You're also losing out if you never come across her *Complete Book of Dragons,* never sample the non-magical and very funny series of books about the Bastable children.

But none of these is my subject. I *had* intended to talk about one of her magical books, *The Phoenix and the Carpet.* It contains not only the sand fairy but also a remarkably conceited phoenix and a threadbare but speedy magic carpet. My favorite Nesbit, I thought. I was wrong. Rereading her a few months ago, I realized that my favorite is a book that belongs to neither series and also has no dragons. No real ones, anyway. It's called *The Railway Children.*

It takes place in rural England about 1905. The main characters are the three children in an upper-middle-class family. The father is a civil servant, apparently fairly high up in the Foreign Office. The mother, who is gifted, writes verse, and occasionally a story, but she doesn't publish. Her audience is her family. And the children? Roberta, called Bobbie, is the eldest. She is eleven, and a little more of an empath than most eleven year olds are. Peter, the proud owner of a toy steam engine that really steams, is ten. And Phyllis, called Phil, is a precocious six year old. "These three lucky children always had everything they needed: pretty clothes, good fires, a lovely nursery with heaps of toys, and a Mother Goose wall-paper."

The luck abruptly runs out. As the children perceive it, one day their father simply vanishes. Their mother will tell them nothing except that he is still alive and she hopes that some day he will come back.

Of course they must leave their nice suburban house near London. The mother finds a much smaller and cheaper one in the deep countryside. But even as interstate highways cut gashes through some of the prettiest valleys in the United States right now, so railroads poked through rural England in 1905. From their new house the children can see the main line of the Great Northern and Southern Railway. They can also see the place where the two tracks vanish into a dark tunnel. They are fascinated. It is at this moment, their first morning in the new house, that they become the Railway Children. They get to know Mr. Perks, the porter at the station, and even the lordly Station Master. They hang around the tracks. They venture into the tunnel, Phil with extreme reluctance, since to her the dark portal seems very much like the entrance to a dragon's lair. (Sometimes there is even steam coming out.) They start naming locomotives. One big green one they honor Phil by calling the Green Dragon. It's actually the 9:15 to London.

> "The Green Dragon's going where Father is," said Phyllis; "if it were a really real dragon, we could stop it and ask it to take our love to Father."
> "Dragons don't carry people's love," said Peter; "they'd be above it."

Very soon the children begin to have adventures. By no means are all of them the sort you'd expect nice middle-class children to get mixed up in, back in 1905.

The first one occurs early in June. There have been three cold rainy days in a row, and the house is freezing. It's wet outside. Bobbie asks her mother (who now spends her days in her room with the door closed, writing frantically for money) if she can light a fire. It would be, of course, a coal fire, and the mother says no, they just don't have the money.

From hanging around the station, the children are now familiar with the huge, almost vertical pile of coal that's kept on a siding. It has a white stripe painted all the way around, just below the top. And that, Mr. Perks explains to Peter, is "To mark how much coal there be, so we'll know if anyone nicks it. So don't you go off with none in your pockets, young gentleman!"

So much coal. And it would take so little to warm their

small house. And these children, remember, have been used to good fires all their lives.

Peter, who's just as imaginative as Bobbie and Phil, decides that if he scales the great pile and digs a little coal right out of the middle, this would be coal-mining, not coal-stealing. Also, they'd never miss it.

His sisters see that he is planning something, but he will not tell them what. "The only reason why I won't tell you," he finally explains, "is because it may be wrong, and I don't want to drag you into it."

In a typical Victorian kid's book, and maybe in a modern one, too, this would be the ideal moment for Bobbie to speak up for honesty. That is not her approach: "'Don't you do it if it's wrong, Peter,' said Bobbie: 'let me do it.'"

As it works out, Peter does do all the stealing, or mining, but both sisters assist in the nightly transport, using a battered pram that once contained baby Phil. All goes well for a week, and then Peter is caught. At this point the English class system helps him. He *is* a young gentleman, even if just now the family has no money, and the Station Master is willing not to prosecute, knowing that a gentleman, or even a gentleboy, will keep his word when he promises to mine no more. The children don't even have to return the week's haul.

Other adventures follow thick and fast, much faster than mere pedestrian plausibility would permit. For example, the three of them happen to be playing, rather dangerously, on the steep hillside near the tunnel entrance when there's a landslide. A mass of trees and rocks falls right on the tracks. By now they know the timetable of up and down trains pretty much by heart. The 11:29 is due in a few minutes; there is not time to run all the way to the station and give warning.

Bobbie comes up with the solution. She and Phil are dressed as young gentlewomen were on cool days in 1905, which means that both are wearing flannel petticoats. Phil is hot, and wishes out loud she could take hers off. Bobbie at that second recalls that what's under their skirts is *red* flannel, which will make excellent danger flags. She and Phil whip their petticoats off, then and there, tear them up, make six red flags, and save the train. E. Nesbit goes into no detail of the disrobing—there's no whiff of kiddie porn, but neither is there the faintest Victorian shock. What, young ladies stripping in public?

I think it's the combination of innocence and honesty on the part of all three children, even as they almost always behave unconventionally, that makes the book such a delight to read. The mother is like that, too. In one of the adventures they bring home a foreigner they found in a distressed state at the station. He speaks no English, and he has somehow lost his railway ticket. The Station Master is just about to call the police when the children intercede. They are confident that their mother will be able to talk to him— and so she can. In the French most educated Europeans spoke in 1905.

He turns out to be a Russian writer, fresh from a Siberian prison. His offense: writing a book the government didn't like. He is pale and sick. The mother instantly takes him into the house, never mind that she is a young and attractive woman, with no trace of a chaperon. In fact, she gives him her bedroom, because it's the warmest.

After he has gone to bed, the mother tells the three children his story. She concludes with his escape from Siberia and his instantly coming to England, where he thinks his family may have taken refuge:

> "How did he get away?" asks Peter.
>
> "When the war came [the Russo-Japanese war of 1904], some of the Russian prisoners were allowed to volunteer as soldiers. And he volunteered. But he deserted the first chance he got and—"
>
> "But that's very cowardly, isn't it"—said Peter—"to desert? Especially when it's war."

"Do you think he owed anything to a country that had done *that* to him?" his mother answers. "If he did, he owed more to his wife and children."

The wonder is that a book with ideas like this should have been so popular in England ninety years ago.

Three children, as in this book, or five children, as in the sand fairy books, are usually the significant numbers for E. Nesbit. There are excellent reasons. Three because she bore three herself. (One of them two months after her first marriage.) Five because two other children became part of the family. *Their* mother was Edith's good friend Alice Hoatson, and their father was the sole man of the house, Edith's husband. A true ménage à trois, just like a French play. The three adults did concede this much to convention: They gave out that Edith had simply adopted little Rosamond and John, and that Alice Hoatson was not their mother, she was just Aunt Alice, who lived in the house as maiden aunts did then. Some maiden.

At the end of *The Railway Children* the father comes back. He turns out to have been in prison, too. As a spy. He had been convicted of selling state secrets to the Russians, but in actual fact had been framed by one of his own staff. The mother wouldn't tell her children where he was because of the disgrace: a father in prison. To that extent she accepted the mores of 1905.

There is a movie of the book, made in 1971. It's a pretty good movie, too, made lovingly. It uses much of Nesbit's wonderful dialogue. It's full of gorgeous locomotives and appealing children (even if Bobbie *does* look more like sixteen than eleven). But for a book that so celebrates unconventionality, it's oddly tame. Bobbie and Phil not only don't help with the transport of stolen coal, Bobbie's instant and firm response, when she finds out what he is doing, is that Peter must return every lump. She says it quickly, though; the whole embarrassing scene is gotten over as fast as possible.

The mother has no good words to say about desertion in time of war—indeed, the Russian no longer deserts. And so on. E. Nesbit dared be, and was, far more radical a hundred years ago than the moviemakers could quite manage in 1971. It may have something to do with size of intended audience.

The Railway Children.
E. Nesbit. 1906.

❧ 22 ❧

The Empty Castle

ICTURE A six hundred-year-old castle in southern England. Give it a moat. On an ancient mound nearby, put Belmotte Tower, the last remnant of a still older castle.

Now, inside the castle put no furniture at all, except a few pieces from junk shops. I'll explain why in a minute. Provide no electricity, either, even though the year is 1935, and you can see the lights twinkle in the little village a mile away. But do sketch in six human figures: the Mortmain family and their one solitary retainer.

The Mortmains of Godsend Castle are an interesting group. The father is a handsome man in his forties. Once a distinguished writer, he is now a semi-recluse who spends nearly all his time holed up in the gate tower. He reads detective stories and does crosswords. The mother—but there is no mother. Instead there's a stepmother, a twenty-nine-year-old ex-model named Topaz who has long pale hair to her waist and ambitions to be an intellectual.

Then there are three children, plus the retainer. I'll take them in ascending order of importance. Thomas, the only son, is a boy of fifteen. He is bright and nice—and he plays a very minor role in the action. Then comes Stephen Colly, the retainer. People in the 1990s tend automatically to put the adjective "aged" in front of retainer, but actually they came in all ages. Stephen is no bent figure shuffling in with the tea; he's a good-looking boy of eighteen. His mother used to be the family maid, and when she died, leaving no visible relatives, it just seemed natural for him to stay on at the castle. He plays a major role, especially late in the book when he is "discovered" by a rich woman from London.

Next comes Rose, the elder daughter. She is beautiful, intensely practical, mad about clothes, and twenty years old. She is co-heroine of the book. By American standards of 1997, she's a bit unusual, because she's never had a boy-friend. This is not because she isn't dying to, though, but because they are so isolated in the castle. And this is England, of course. It would have to be someone of her own class.

Finally, there's Cassandra Mortmain, age seventeen. By any standards, Cassandra is an unusual girl. She's twice as imaginative and three times as alive as most human beings. Even Rose's hunger for experience, adventure, men, etc., is feeble compared to Cassandra's. She is not only co-heroine, she narrates the entire book, and that is one of its greatest charms. Cassandra's mode of narration is (1) romantic, (2) funny, (3) full of insight, and (4) what any teenage girl would be proud to come up with, if she happened to be a brilliant writer. By this I mean that Cassandra sounds au-thentic—and authentically seventeen. There is no hint of Dodie Smith, the adult author, manipulating her behind the scenes. It is truly Cassandra's book.

But enough. You have been waiting impatiently to learn why these people live almost without furniture. It's for the same reason that clothes-loving Rose has about three dresses, and that the whole family (plus Stephen) are per-petually hungry. They have run out of money.

They can't sell the castle, because they don't own it. Back when the father was getting huge royalties—espe-cially from America, where his book *Jacob Wrestling* was a bestseller—he rented the castle on a forty-year lease. At the moment he hasn't paid the rent in three years, and piece by piece they have sold all the furniture. Remember that 1935 was the depth of the Great Depression, and it was not unusual to have run out of money.

As the book opens, it's twilight of an April day. Rose is in the kitchen, ironing her only nightgown. Stephen Colly is pumping up water from the cistern in the castle courtyard. Thomas is still at school. Mr. Mortmain is holed up in the gate tower. Topaz is bending over the kitchen fire, blowing; the weather is rainy and the castle is very cold. As for Cassandra, she is sitting in the kitchen sink, recording the scene in her diary.

The *sink?* Why there? Because not only does the castle lack electricity, the Mortmains can't afford many candles, and the sink's in front of the only window where there's enough light left to write by. Anyway, Cassandra likes to put things picturesquely. As she soon admits, it's really only her feet that are in the sink: "The rest of me is on the draining board, which I have padded with our dog's blanket and the tea-cosy."

A number of things soon happen. Stephen Colly, having finished pumping the water, comes in and shyly hands Cassandra yet another of the poems he keeps copying out of anthologies and giving to her. Thomas, home from school, checks the henhouse and finds the hens have resumed laying, which means they'll get an egg each for dinner, instead of just bread and margarine. Rose and Topaz have a sharp quarrel over money. Rose wants Topaz to go back to London and resume posing for artists. Topaz doesn't want to be away from her husband. Besides, she says, the artist who pays her best clearly thinks of her as a sex object:

> "I've had more trouble with him than I should care to let your father know."
>
> Rose said, "I should have thought it was worth while to have a little trouble in order to earn some real money."
>
> "Then *you* have the trouble, dear," said Topaz.

This infuriates Rose, who's longing to have that kind of trouble, and sees no prospects. She flings her head back dramatically and says, "It may interest you to know that for some time now, I've been considering selling myself. If necessary, I shall go on the streets."

Cassandra, from the sink, points out that this will be hard to do in rural Suffolk. Rose sees that.

"But if Topaz will kindly lend me the fare to London and give me a few hints—"

Rose doesn't, of course, sell herself in London. Instead, Stephen gets a job, at 25 shillings a week, on a nearby farm. And soon after that the Americans come. The Americans are two brothers, Simon and Neil Cotton, who one dark evening blunder up the muddy track that leads to the castle. Both are husband material. All sorts of adventures follow.

I Capture the Castle is a hard book to classify. It is much too funny to be merely a teen romance, or merely any kind of romance. It's much too seriously romantic to be a spoof, a burlesque, or the kind of book they call "rollicking." In fact, it's much too individual and much too well written to be labeled at all.

Except maybe with one label that says, "Contents: 100% Pure Delight." And another that says, "Warning: This style may prove addictive."

That's a real danger. Because if you, as teenage girl or man of fifty-three, read *I Capture the Castle,* and fall in love with it, you will naturally want to go on to more. There is no more. Dodie Smith wrote numerous other books, including the one the Disney factory adapted for *101 Dalmatians,* and some are better than others. But *I Capture the Castle* is her only masterpiece. I don't say that derogatively. After all, how many writers have produced even one?

I Capture the Castle.
Dodie Smith. 1948.

✣ 23 ✣

Prince of Deira

STEPHEN, PRINCE OF DEIRA, has ridden out from the castle alone. For three days now he has been following a mysterious white deer through the forest. He is only fifteen, and still careless. Wearing the golden fillet round his head that reveals him as a prince, he has come right up to the invisible boundary that marks the beginning of the neighboring kingdom of Bernicia. In fact, he has gone twelve paces across it. An older boy, Aella's son, Prince of Bernicia, is waiting among the dark trees to capture him. Stephen will be used, probably, as a living shield the next time King Aella goes to war. That is, he will be on the king's horse, hands tied, propped in front of the king, so that his body will first receive any weapon.

What is this? Another sword-and-sorcery adventure? Some older but little-known fairy tale? Neither. It's the opening of a historical novel for pre-adolescents and early adolescents—a wonderful, grim, romantic, and deeply truthful novel, full of pain and joy. It's like no other novel for children that I know.

Deira and Bernicia, though to my ear they sound like places you might find in Portugal, are in fact parts of England. Were, anyway. What is now southern Yorkshire was once the kingdom of Deira. What is now northern Yorkshire was once Bernicia.

In the year 674 both were Christian kingdoms, though plenty of paganism and some magic survived. The great cathedral at York already existed, and there were rich monasteries scattered through both countries. One of them contained a saint. Caedmon, the illiterate farm laborer who became the first Christian poet of England, was then living in the monastery of Whitby, in Bernicia.

Within this historical setting Lolah Burford has composed something pretty close to a masterpiece. Being a true scholar of Anglo-Saxon, she evokes the seventh century with great power. You feel and respond to the high culture of the time, where a small harp might be passed from hand to hand after dinner in the hall of a manor house, and every person at the table was expected to sing a song "on some high subject." Not just the gentry at the top of the table, but the lowliest farmhand at the bottom. It was in such a hall that Caedmon the cowherd discovered his poetic calling.

You also experience the terrible brutality of the time: the routine use of torture, even by a king on his son; the capture and enslavement or death that would follow if you left the narrow territory of your petty kingdom without some pretty careful arrangements.

Stephen, of course, made no arrangements at all before he unwittingly crossed the border. He survived anyway. That's because neither he nor Aella's son fully accept their fathers' bloodthirsty doctrines of war. What happens is that the two boys find themselves liking each other, and presently thinking that if they ruled instead of their fathers, the two kingdoms would be at peace.

The one boy impulsively decides to break all rules and let the other go. Before he can, one of his own men rides up. Aella's son can hardly explain that he's planning to release an enemy. His father would think that treason. Instead he works out a charade in which Stephen can seem to escape. But the boys have talked too long. War is imminent, and the border is full of scouts. The two princes find themselves surrounded by a group of Stephen's men, and now Stephen must pretend that the other boy is a Bernician serf he has caught. He must take him back to the castle for questioning. And that evening, moved both by love and by a sense of honor (he should himself at this minute be on the rack in Aella's castle), he must contrive his new friend's escape—knowing as he does so how terrible the consequences will be for him.

All that is prelude, a brilliant prelude, to the main action of the book. Naturally Stephen's father is outraged at the escape of an enemy who has seen the inside of his castle, and that on the eve of war. He asks his son to explain. Stephen quite literally cannot explain in any terms that his father would understand, and he does not try. He resigns himself to the limb-breaking torture that his father sadly and, yes, lovingly commands. And at a moment that night when he faints from the pain, the principal movement of the book begins.

When Stephen faints, his spirit leaves his body. It travels in time, not space. More than a thousand years later, near the site of his father's castle, a Yorkshire baronet has his country house. Sir Joseph is a stern father, too, though only by the milder standards of 1822. Sir Joseph has a twelve-year-old daughter named Margery, a girl as imaginative and as quick as Stephen himself. Like reaching to like, Stephen appears as a ghost to Margery. At first he is visible only to her and her small brother Peter—and when Margery tells her parents about the strange boy, she is severely punished for telling lies.

The rest of the book jumps back and forth between 674 and 1822, as Stephen himself does. When he is able to be with Margery and Peter, he tells them—and the reader, of course—about his own time. He has known Caedmon; as a small boy he had been in Whitby monastery himself, to be taught by the monks. He hasn't known Grendel, but Beowulf's story he has heard often, and tells it as it would seem to someone in the seventh century. When Margery wonders how he can speak to her in modern English, he quite matter-of-factly tells her how the gift of tongues came to him through an enchanted fish in a pool in Ireland, where he had gone with his father in an earlier war.

What eventually happens to Stephen, either in 674 or in 1822, I am not about to reveal. It is enough to say that it is superbly imagined, as everything in this book is. There is not a false note in the whole two hundred pages.

I will say, however, what happened to Stephen's book in 1968, and that is a story romantic in itself. At that time Ms. Burford had written four novels, and published none. She was in London, and sick. As impulsively as Aella's son deciding to free Stephen, she decided that if the book were ever published, she would give all the royalties to Deira. That is, to the great cathedral in York. It is not the one Stephen knew, the one his great-grandfather built. That was destroyed by the Normans. One piece of wall remains, of which Stephen might have touched a stone. No matter. The present York Minster, though a mere seven hundred years old, is glory enough for any city.

The Vision of Stephen did get published—in New York in 1972, and in London the next year. Lolah Burford kept the promise she had made herself. It is glorious that through her agency the Prince of Deira traveled forward in time still further, and has now contributed some two thousand pounds to the great church his ancestors founded.

The Vision of Stephen.
Lolah Burford. 1972.

⊸⟋ *24* ⟍⊷

A Strange Voyage

I

IN THE YEAR 1834 a small English expedition set out for Africa. It was led by the world's top authority on animal language, Doctor John Dolittle. There were seven other members of the party, plus a stowaway who showed up after they had put to sea. These nine formed, by a wide margin, the most unusual group of explorers ever to set out from England.

The venture started well. Their ship, a well-built sloop, made a fast crossing, and only six weeks after leaving England they were in sight of the African coast. But here their luck changed. So violent a storm blew up that their ship got dashed to pieces on the rocks. All nine expedition members made it safely to land, only to be captured by the local ruler, who was no mere chieftain but a king. They explained to the king that all they sought was passage through his territory; their actual destination lay deep in the interior. He coldly refused them:

> "Many years ago," he said, "a white man came to these shores, and I was very kind to him. But after he had dug holes in the ground to get the gold, and killed all the elephants to get their ivory tusks, he

went away secretly in his ship—without so much as saying 'Thank you.' Never again shall a white man travel through the lands of Jolliginki."

He then claps eight of the nine into prison. The ninth stays free only because the king is unaware of her.

They don't stay in prison long. The ninth member of the expedition, who is a 183-year-old parrot named Polynesia, liberates them that very night. She had concealed herself during the royal hearing precisely because she feared the king might have jail in mind.

Once free, they hurry toward the interior, soon pursued by the king's soldiers and by the queen in person. If all the members of the expedition had been able to travel as fast as Doctor Dolittle and Polynesia, they might have got over the border without further incident. But all were not. One of the explorers is a small pig named Gub-Gub, and he is not only timid, even a touch cowardly, he tires easily. Doctor Dolittle often has to carry him. Only the extraordinary Bridge of Apes (a living bridge) saves them from recapture.

II

If my stratagem worked, for the first sentence or two you thought I was talking about an historical event. What I'm actually talking about is the first of the twelve Doctor Dolittle books written by Hugh Lofting between 1920 and 1947. They are wonderfully funny absurdist stories, with only very occasional touches of reality.

They have their origin in the trenches of World War I. Hugh Lofting was an Anglo-Irish engineer who had settled in America with an American wife. But World War I was a hard war to stay out of. That's how it got its name. Lofting wound up going back to Britain to become a captain in the Irish Guards, and then being shipped off to fight. At that point two things came together to produce Doctor Dolittle and his parrot, pig, crocodile, etc. One was that Lofting needed subject matter for letters home to his children. He wasn't about to tell them anything about the horrible reality of trench warfare; he wanted something loving and funny that would make small children giggle.

The other thing was his horror at the military treatment of animals. Armies then still had a substantial animal element—not only the high-bred horses of the cavalry, but artillery horses, mules, even some camels. What shocked Captain Lofting was that a wounded horse or mule was rarely treated by a vet; instead it was summarily shot. (People who know Bill Mauldin's great World War II cartoon book *Up Front* may recall the drawing of an old cavalry sergeant whose jeep has broken down. He has his pistol out, and with averted eyes is about to shoot the jeep through the hood.)

Lofting proceeded to invent a physician—John Dolittle, M.D.—who gradually ceases to treat human beings at all, and spends his entire time healing animals. There's a serious component here, since Lofting really did think animals had a stronger claim on life and on medical attention than World War I gave them, but it is well hidden under layers of the kinds of absurdity calculated to keep a small child laughing.

Similarly, there is a serious component to the king of the Jolliginki's indignant account of the white man who came and took all the gold and ivory. Lofting, who had worked as an engineer in West Africa before he came to the U.S., was obviously no great proponent of colonialism. But he *was* a great proponent of broad humor, from which African royalty was in no way exempt.

Lofting did his own illustrations for the Dolittle books— as he had originally done them for the letters home—and he spared nobody: man, woman, or beast. He drew an absurd African king. He also drew an absurd John Dolittle—a stubby little man with a nose like a potato. He drew a funny-looking African queen—her improbable name is Er-mintrude—and an even funnier-looking English spinster. Miss Sarah Dolittle is Dr. D's sister, and until the advent of the crocodile, who liked to nap under her bed, she used to keep house for him. The unusual two-headed animal known as a pushmi-pullyu is pretty silly, too, though not quite as ridiculous as the giant asparagus trees that appear in one of the later books. (In the matter of oversize vegetables, Lofting was about thirty years ahead of Woody Allen.)

In short, I think it's fair to say that everything and everybody in the Dolittle books is treated absurdly—and the great strength of the books is that the humor is both broad enough to be obvious (mostly) to a six year old and subtle enough to tickle adults. The uncanny resemblance of Gub-Gub's behavior to what one might expect if a three-year-old human child had been on the expedition would be lost on neither.

But we need a larger example. I'll use the way in which Lofting handles the outfitting of the expedition.

The African trip has its start when Dr. D gets a message that a plague has struck African monkeys, and they desperately need help. Of course he is willing to go.

But this was 1834. No flights to Lagos, no steamer service. The first problem is how to get a ship. In fact, how to get a free ship. Dr. D has no money at all; what he had back when he treated human beings he has long since spent on animals. He thinks hard. Then he says, "I knew a seaman once who brought his baby to me with measles. Maybe he'll lend us his boat—the baby got well."

The sailor is delighted to lend his large and roomy sloop. Dr. D and the animals begin to stock her. Polynesia (you might think of her parrot-wise as Polly Nesia) has been to sea before, and gives lots of advice:

"You must have plenty of pilot bread," she says. "'Hardtack' they call it. And you must have beef in cans—and an anchor."

"I expect the ship will have its own anchor," said the Doctor.

"Well, make sure," said Polynesia. "Because it's very important. You can't stop if you haven't got an anchor. And you'll need a bell."

"What's that for?" asked the Doctor.

"To tell the time by," said the parrot. "You go and ring it every half hour, and then you know what time it is."

Some of the jokes here will go over the head of a six year old, and some won't. But the general absurdity will be clear. And the book is pretty sure to delight.

III

There is one more thing to tell about Doctor Dolittle. His adventures are available in two versions. In one of them the Jolliginki are clearly black. Indeed, Polynesia, who like so many parrots has rather a foul mouth, occasionally uses a racial epithet when talking about them. In the other version they are colorless. They belong to no race in particular. In the version I've been quoting, which is the original, the person who made off with the gold and ivory is unequivocally white. In the revised version he is just "a man."

Why is this? It's because in the 1960s Doctor Dolittle became controversial. A group called the Council on Interracial Books for Children denounced the book as racist to the core. I'm not sure about *that,* but it is certainly true that Bumpo, crown prince of Jolliginki, grew up addicted to European fairy tales, and since he wants to enter one and find Sleeping Beauty, he has often wished he were a white rather than a black prince. He is like the French novelist and naval officer Pierre Loti, who was short and dark and who would have preferred to be tall and blond. "I am not my type," Loti once lamented.

The consequence of the denunciation was that Dolittle books rather quickly vanished from lists of books recommended to be bought for schools and libraries. This wasn't censorship; Lofting's publisher remained perfectly free to sell the books, and any school or library that wanted to could buy them. But many fewer did want to. One by one the books went out of print.

Then in 1988 a new publisher brought *The Story of Doctor Dolittle* back into print. Lofting himself had been dead for forty years. But his son Christopher was around, and so was the sister-in-law who had worked with him on his last few books. These two, with the help of three editors at Dell, expurgated Dr. D.

They did an excellent job. I have just one quibble. I think it was silly to take out the words "black" and "white." We are, after all. But the revised version is just as funny as the original; it's merely a few pages shorter. Should you buy the book, you probably ought to get the new version. But there would be nothing terribly sinful about going to a second-hand bookstore and picking up a copy of one of the fifty or so previous impressions.

The Story of Doctor Dolittle.
Hugh Lofting. 1920.

❧ 25 ❧

An Animal Epic

TWENTY YEARS AGO it would not have been necessary to call anyone's attention to Richard Adam's novel *Watership Down*. It had been published in England to much acclaim, and when it reached this country it not only made the best-seller list, it led it. Parents all over the country were giving the book to their children. Children were sneakily reading it under the covers with flashlights. And they were looking at pet rabbits with a new eye, perhaps learning a few words of the language called Lapine.

In my own house, my stepdaughter Kiki and I became addicts. We read the entire book aloud, taking turns. It's long, though not as long as we wished it were. In daily life we used rabbit terminology whenever possible. "Let's *silflay*," we'd say, instead of "Let's get something to eat." We spoke of the *hrududu*, not the car.

To surprise this surprise-loving little girl, I even spent $25 and got a Lapine vanity plate for my own hrududu. HRAKA, it read, which is mildly scatalogical, the rabbit term for rabbit droppings. It was noticed at once. We got double and even triple takes from the drivers of other *hrududil*, followed by honks, waving, actual cheers. Rarely indeed does a book as good as *Watership Down* prove such an overwhelming success.

But that was long ago. The success of a wonderful book

in the early seventies doesn't ensure that children will hear anything about it now. Nor does the movie made in 1978 do much—not for the book it doesn't. The book is heroic fantasy. The film is an animated cartoon. They don't mix. Animated cartoons lend themselves readily to the simpler forms of humor, and, in the hands of Disney, to cuteness. They can also handle adventure, provided you stay on the surface. But depth is beyond them, as is grandeur.

The classic case is *The Lord of the Rings*—as a book the greatest heroic fantasy of this century, as animated cartoon a piece of junk. (Movie rankers usually give it no stars at all, just that insulting symbol, a turkey.) The cartoon of *Watership Down* is no turkey—it has considerable artistic pretensions—but it gives children neither the immense narrative force of the book nor any sense that life has high possibilities.

Watership Down is a rabbit epic. As the book opens, a yearling rabbit named Hazel (a male, named for the species of tree) is debating whether to leave his warren and trek across England in search of a new home. He is restive in the warren, both because there are too many bucks and not enough does and because a kind of Lapine police force known as the *owsla* is so bossy. The heaviest males, those best able to wound or kill another rabbit, generally form the warren police, and they do not allow many privileges to the yearlings.

But what decides Hazel to go is a sort of vision that another rabbit has. Don't smile. Many animals have what to humans seem to be uncanny responses. Dogs, for example, often sense weather changes in advance of the weather channel. Many dogs can also detect strong emotion in their owners, no matter how well hidden the owner supposes it to be, and sometimes the dog knows that violence is coming even before the about-to-be-violent person knows it.

But back to rabbits. The other rabbit is a small buck named Fiver, the runt of Hazel's litter. Most wild rabbits are fearful a lot of the time, and Fiver is more fearful than most. He gets his vision when he and Hazel are silflaying near the entrance to the field where the warren has its burrows. Human beings have just been there, and have erected a large sign. Neither rabbit can read it, of course. But both can smell a combination of rank man-odor, oily machine-smell from the hrududu the workmen came in, and even a little tobacco-stink where one of them ground out a cigarette.

Hazel merely dislikes all this, but Fiver goes into a panic, almost an epileptic fit. It seems to him as if the field is covered in blood. (Hazel more prosaically sees the field tinted red by the setting sun.) Fiver is so earnest that he convinces his brother that the whole warren is in danger, as indeed it is. What the sign announces is the immediate development of the field into housing lots. This will bring on the kind of hrududil we call bulldozers. Goodbye, warren.

Hazel now attempts to persuade the rest of the rabbits to migrate. Don't smile at that, either. Even with creatures as minimally individual as honeybees, there are times when the minority in a hive want to swarm and the majority are not willing. Something fairly close to wordless argument takes place.

In the end, eleven rabbits leave the warren, all male. Two have been members of the owsla, and they of course are good fighters. One of them, a particularly appealing rabbit named Bigwig, is going to be second only to Hazel in the adventures that follow.

And what adventures they are! On the first day out they have to cross a river that's as big to them as the Hudson is to us. With some brilliant improvisation by a rabbit named Blackberry, all eleven make it across. On the far side Hazel finds a bean field where they can feed and rest. But crows use that field, too, and very soon a crow is trying to kill the weak little rabbit Pipkin. It uses the favorite crow technique of stabbing for the eyes with its beak. Between them the two former owsla, Bigwig and Silver, drive the crow off, but it is a close call.

Events now follow with the same sweep as in any epic. The eleven travelers find another warren, and are dazzled. The rabbits here look bigger and glossier than any they have ever seen. When invited to join, they gladly move in.

But the new warren turns out to be a place of death. It is, in fact, managed by a human farmer. The rabbits are wild. They dug the burrows—or, rather, their ancestors did. But the farmer feeds them. Instead of composting his carrot scrapings, spoiled turnips, etc., he dumps them regularly in the field in front of the warren for the rabbits to eat. They are marvelously well fed. He also harvests rabbits every week, using snares. Bigwig nearly dies, caught in one.

Later they come to a second warren. Here the owsla has become a paramilitary organization. Everyone obeys strict rules, and no one is allowed to leave. How the twelve of them fight their way out is perhaps the most exciting part of the book. (How *twelve?* A rabbit named Strawberry from the death warren has joined them.)

The real-world adventures are no better, though, than the five interpolated stories that the rabbits themselves tell when they're holed up underground on a rainy day, or when they need calming after a great danger. All concern the legendary figure El-ahrairah, whose name translates Prince with a Thousand Enemies, or just Prince Rabbit. I had forgotten in the many years since reading with Kiki just how fine these rabbit myths are. Just as I had forgotten how many funny things Bigwig says in the course of the book— without ever compromising his role as a principal hero.

A book like this could easily have become allegory, as Orwell's *Animal Farm* actually did. The characters in Orwell's book wear animal skins, but are human underneath, with just one or two animal traits.

Not Adams's. One of the glories of the book is that it stays almost entirely true to rabbit behavior while still telling an anthropomorphic story. Yes, Adams makes his animals talk, and they can talk across species lines, though with an accent. This never bothered Kiki for a second. It delighted her. Her favorite line in the whole book is spoken by an injured seagull named Kehaar. The rabbits have found him, and he thinks they are going to attack. "I 'urt you like damn," he warns Hazel, raising his still-formidable beak. When Kiki wasn't speaking actual Lapine, she was apt to be addressing that line of Kehaar's to the cat, or to me if I didn't want to read with her at that minute.

But in this language, which rabbits don't really have, Adams has them discuss only behavior that rabbits really exhibit. Mostly, anyway. They never *do* pass hraka underground. The females *do* dig nearly all the holes, though males will make halfhearted scrapes in an emergency. A big rabbit *will* as a matter of course drive a smaller rabbit away from a favorite foodstuff—say a cowslip—and eat it himself. As far as we know, rabbits don't refer to moonrise as Inlé, but it really is a moment of great significance for them.

You would hardly turn to Bugs Bunny for insights on animal behavior, still less for any clue on how best to live. But you would turn to *Watership Down*. Considering that you also get a true epic, finely observed landscape, a gripping plot, any amount of good dialogue, and five legends that all by themselves would make an excellent book, I think you would have to conclude that you had been reading a masterpiece.

Watership Down.
Richard Adams. 1972.

✒ 26 ✑

Last Woman Meets Last Man

FOR AT LEAST five thousand years, human beings have been telling stories about the end of our race. Well, not quite the end, usually, but an abrupt reduction to a mere handful or even to a single couple. In the Bible, it's Noah and his family who alone survive the flood that God sends to punish us—and who then are permitted to start the race over. In Greek mythology, it's Pyrrha and her husband Deucalion who alone survive the flood sent by Zeus to punish us, and who are permitted to begin anew.

By the time Mary Shelley did her version of the story in 1826 (a few years after she wrote *Frankenstein*), God no longer played a part, and the extinction was not punishment, just bad luck. In Shelley's novel *The Last Man,* it's a naturally occurring plague that reduces America to nothing, London to a village of a few hundred people, and finally produces Last Man, a fellow named Lionel. At the end of the book he sails off in a small boat, hopeful that somewhere in the world he will find Last Woman and that they will then start us up again.

In our own time, not only God but also nature has usually dropped out of the story. Now it is we who destroy ourselves. In most doomsday novels we manage this by fighting a nuclear war, though occasionally some writer prefers to have a virus escape from a lab, or get deliberately loosed by a mad scientist. Either way, we die.

Clearly, near-extinction is a scenario that grips the human mind, and clearly it is one that we do not see as entirely bad. To witness the deaths of five or six billion people, innocent babies and all, is to witness an appalling tragedy. But to meet Last Man and Last Woman is quite exciting. Our trouble-prone race is being given a second chance, with a new Adam and Eve. Maybe they will do better than the first pair.

One of the best last-man books is, surprisingly, written for children. Big children. Teenagers. It's called *Z for Zachariah*—and if Adam gets the first letter of the alphabet and is First Man, you can easily guess what man Zachariah is. The author, who wrote under the name Robert C. O'Brien, is well-known, but almost entirely for one book. He won the Newbery Medal in 1972 with *Mrs. Frisby and the Rats of NIMH*, which is also worth giving to a teenager. But I think *Zachariah* is a shade better.

The book opens about a year after a war in which both sides used not only nuclear warheads and viruses, but also plague bacilli, nerve gas, anything they can think of that will hurt or kill human beings. They are extremely successful. Almost all of us are killed, and almost the entire world becomes uninhabitable.

One exception is a small valley in what might be Kentucky. This valley, completely ringed by mountains, is a meteorological enclave; that is, it has its own weather system. It received only a little fallout and nerve gas. Equally important, one of the two brooks in the valley rises from a deep spring, and its first few hundred yards are not contaminated. You can drink from it and not die.

The whole book is a journal kept by Last Woman—who is actually Last Girl. She lives in that valley. She is a self-reliant and completely lovable fifteen year old named Ann

Burden. She was fourteen when the war—it lasted only a week—took place.

Ann has been alone ever since. She has no parents, no siblings, no friends. She has no radio to listen to, or, rather she does have one, but there are no stations still broadcasting. She has no TV, no videos to rent, no emergency phone number to call, no adult to give her help of any kind.

What happened to her family? Just a day or two after the war ended, her father, brother, and cousin took the farm pickup and drove to Ogdentown, twenty-five miles away. Everybody was dead. The next day, still hoping to find other survivors, and not understanding the risks they took, they venture to the nearest city. This time her mother goes, too, while Ann stays home in case someone should show up in the valley.

The radiation her family got on that second trip is enough to kill them all, and it does. Ann is not only alone but trapped. Her little valley is a green island, surrounded on all sides by gray, lifeless, radioactive woods. There are no birds except for a few crows that were smart enough or lucky enough to stay in the valley and never fly over the deadly hills. It is possible that there are other green islands of life, but even if Ann knew for sure there were one just fifty miles away, she couldn't get there, any more than Robinson Crusoe could have swum home to England.

So Ann, who if there had been no war would have been a carefree tenth grader at Ogdentown High School, must do everything kids usually count on grown-ups for. One of the pleasures of the book is seeing how she learns to cope with a world where there is no electricity, no packaged food except for a dwindling supply of canned goods, no rules except whatever she makes for herself. She has other problems as well.

On the first page of the book, Ann sees something both exciting and scary: smoke from what is obviously someone's campfire, up in the dead hills. Three evenings she sees it, always closer. Someone is coming slowly along what once was State Highway 9.

Ann has, of course, been horribly lonely. When she first sees the smoke, she is thrilled to think that someone else is alive. But she is also terrified. "Suppose a car came over the hill," she writes in her journal, "and I ran out, and whoever was in it got out—suppose he was crazy? Or suppose it was someone mean, or even cruel, and brutal? A murderer? What could I do?"

As a result of that fear, she decides to hide and to observe the maker of the campfire before she shows herself. Before he arrives (she always assumes it's a man) she hastily puts things in disarray, so he won't instantly realize someone is living in the valley. Then she takes her father's binoculars and rifle and goes up to a cave she and her brother used to play in.

What she sees when he comes in sight is indeed a man. He is on foot, pulling a heavy wagon. He is wearing a coverall and a helmet with a glass viewplate. As you later learn, he has been walking (cars are radioactive) all the way from Ithaca, New York (he was a research chemist at Cornell), and this is the first island of life he has found.

This man—his name is not Zachariah but John R. Loomis, and he's in his early thirties—makes a terrible mistake less than an hour after he reaches the valley. When he sees the green trees, which, remember, are the first he has seen in a year, he gets not one but two Geiger counters from his wagon. When both report only light background radiation, he takes first his helmet and then his suit off. And then he does something reckless. Having seen minnows in the safe brook as he came down the hill, and not realizing that below the house the two brooks come together and form a radioactive creek, he takes what must be his first bath in a year. And gets radiation sickness, and nearly dies.

He survives because Ann comes out of hiding to nurse him. And as he begins to recover, and they talk, she is impressed with how much he knows and how many good ideas he has for keeping life going in the valley. She begins to imagine their future together. He's more than twice her age; she still thinks of him as "Mr. Loomis," as if he were one of her high school teachers. But clearly he is Adam to her Eve.

One of the most touching passages in the book occurs about two weeks after Loomis arrives. The apple trees in her father's orchard have just come into blossom. "I thought, if I ever got married, apple blossoms are what I would like to have in the church." And then her thought, Eve-like, proceeds:

> When Mr. Loomis recovered from his sickness, there was no reason why we could not plan to be married in a year; that is, next June, perhaps on my seventeenth birthday. I knew there could not be any minister, but the marriage ceremony was all written out in the back of the hymnal.

Last Girl is in the very act of becoming First Woman, and anyone who cares at all about the human race feels happy. But that's not how the book goes. Loomis has different ideas. He means to take over.

Ann did not immediately realize that Mr. Loomis has a controlling personality, because of course he was desperately ill when she came down from the cave. Couldn't even stand up. It's hard to domineer under those circumstances. But as he recovered he began to want absolute obedience. For example, he was able while still convalescent to tell her how to get her father's tractor running. But since there will not be any more gasoline made, probably for a hundred years, he wants sole power to decide when the tractor should be driven. As soon as he can walk, he steals the key.

That she might have accepted. It's not as if there were other marital prospects. But when, once he gets well, he somewhat clumsily attempts to rape her, she retreats to the cave. He hunts her, as one would an animal. She gets hold of the safesuit, meaning to leave the valley. He attempts to shoot her in the ankle, so that she will have to stay there as his lame, obedient wife.

I won't say how it comes out, not caring to spoil the story. I'll just say that it's a *lot* more exciting than the Book of Genesis or Mary Shelley's rather wordy novel about Lionel.

O'Brien, whose real name was Robert Conley, was an editor of *National Geographic,* which is how he came to know about meteorological enclaves and such. He did not take up novel-writing until his forties—and then he died at fifty-five. He had time for only four books, of which Z *for Zachariah* was the last. It was a great way to end.

Z for Zachariah.
Robert C. O'Brien. 1975.

◄§ 27 ?◄

A Dog from Heaven

I

THE PHILOSOPHER Aristotle had an interesting theory of what keeps the planets in their proper courses. To him it seemed obvious that if they were left to themselves they would all shoot off in a straight line, like arrows shot from a bow, and soon be far out of the reach of any school bus. (Well, he didn't say *that,* because he didn't know about school buses.) So what kept them in the solar system? Gods did. Somewhere between forty-seven and fifty-five gods were busy steering. Medieval Christian thinkers, uneasy with all those gods, tended to say no, it was between forty-seven and fifty-five angels.

Even Sir Isaac Newton, a great scientist and a pretty good astronomer, assumed a little bit of power steering when the solar system was first set up: "The motions which the planets now have," he wrote, "could not spring from any natural cause alone but were impressed by an intelligent Agent."

II

About twenty years ago the English writer Diana Wynne Jones took this idea and ran with it. In her fantasy novel

133

for children *Dogsbody,* she supposes that not just the planets but every heavenly body has a resident spirit, who is its ruler. The brighter the star, the more powerful the ruler.

In many ways these sky-rulers resemble oversize human beings. They have bodies, fall in love, get married. Well, not actually *married.* Let's say have long-term and publicly recognized relationships. Here Jones makes clever use of real astronomy.

Aristotle didn't know it, nor Newton, but about half of the visible stars are actually star systems. And many of these, including Sirius, brightest star in the sky, are binary systems. That is, two stars have come so close together that they now revolve around their common center of mass. In fact, they sometimes get so close that one will pass material to the other, causing the other to brighten and perhaps become a nova. If that degree of intimacy reminds you a little of human behavior, it should. What's more, astronomers usually refer to the smaller star in a binary as the big one's companion.

The rulers are like human beings in other ways, too. For example, they can lose their tempers, just as we earthlings do, only with them it's more dramatic. They quite literally flare up. The star gets brighter; thermonuclear clouds may reach out a million miles, as we see with our own sun; occasionally one goes supernova and dies.

One last bit of background. Jones imagines that there is a heavenly court in which rulers who misbehave can be tried. Usually three stars of first magnitude form the court. They have the power to send a fellow star-lord into exile; they can even take his consciousness and transfer it into the body of some far smaller and humbler creature. It's a little like the fate of the high-caste Hindu who for his sins finds himself reincarnated as a mud wasp.

III

As *Dogsbody* opens, court is in session. Sirius, the Dog Star, brightest star in heaven, is on trial. He is charged with having used one of the incredibly powerful weapons known as a Zoi to kill a young luminary from the constellation Gemini, and with then having lost the Zoi. It would be a good deal safer to lose a hydrogen bomb.

Whether he actually committed these crimes isn't clear, though there are hints that he did not. Nevertheless, partly on the evidence of his beautiful Companion, he is found guilty on both counts.

"D-denizen of Sirius," says Polaris, who stammers a little, "You are hereby s-sentenced to be s-stripped of all s-spheres, honors, and eff-ffulgences and banished f-from here to the body of a creature native to that s-sphere where the m-missing Z-zoi is thought to have f-fallen." He will have the lifetime of that creature in which to recover the Zoi; if he fails he will die when the native creature does, and that will be the end of one of the great star-lords.

Where the Zoi is thought to have fallen is on an obscure planet known as Earth. The next thing Sirius knows, he is being born as a puppy, one of a litter of seven in an English kennel. His small puppy brain contains no memory of his real self, though as he grows he gradually recaptures bits and pieces, and finally full awareness. Right now he knows no more than any other newborn pup. And, indeed, even near the end of the book, when he fully understands who he is, he continues to think partly dog-thoughts, and to be partly controlled by his dog's body. The way Jones handles his double nature is one of the many excellences of the book.

Sirius and the other six pups are all mongrels, from a human point of view, and the woman who runs the kennel instantly decides to have them drowned in the river. Two in fact do drown—and Sirius survives only because the

Denizen of our own Sun recognizes him, even in puppy form, and is able to keep him warm and alive until he washes ashore. At this moment the second plot of the book begins. Three children are down playing by the river. One of them sees and rescues the almost-dead puppy. Against the advice of the other two, she takes him home with her.

This child, the heroine of the book, is an Irish girl named Kathleen. You never learn her age, but she seems to be around twelve. Her mother walked out years ago, and is now believed to be in America. Her father is in an Irish jail, a political prisoner. What's she doing in England? Her English uncle has taken her in—and by doing so without even consulting his wife, has ensured that she will not be welcome. (As you get to know his wife, you realize that all the consultation in the world wouldn't have made her much of a friendly stepmom, but he still should have asked.) The other two children are her English cousins Basil and Robin. Basil dislikes her, as he does all things Irish; Robin is quite fond of her, but he is only a little boy, and has scant influence in the family.

Duffie, the stepmother, is coldly rejecting when Kathleen turns up with the puppy. "Take the filthy little beast outside and drown it," she orders. But by promising to do all the cooking and all the cleaning, Kathleen wins a reprieve.

That temporarily takes care of Duffie, but there are three other members of the household from whom Sirius must win acceptance. Duffie has three cats. They are among the most charming and interesting cats in literature, especially the elegant and fast-thinking Tibbles. Considering just how loaded with cats literature is, that's a high claim. But a true one. If there were nothing at all in this book except the story of how a puppy came to be accepted by three cats who initially hated him, it would still be a wonderful book.

But of course there is a great deal else. The characters include not only three cats and numerous dogs (the

Denizen of Sol was able to save four of Sirius's litter mates from drowning, and you meet them all), but also a mother fox and her cubs. You meet not only a dozen or so human beings, but also as many luminaries. The spirit who has been ruling Sirius's sector of heaven since the banishment, and who is usually spoken of as New-Sirius and addressed as Your Effulgency, that spirit visits Earth, along with the beautiful Companion. (About this point you learn who really killed the young luminary.)

Still more, the Denizen of the planet Earth plays a key role as the search for the Zoi mounts in intensity, and even the denizen of our moon has a cameo part. *Dogsbody* is a wonderful, exciting, high-serious drama, which also has many funny scenes, especially with the cats, and with the Denizen of Sol. This relatively low-ranking but bold luminary works throughout the book to help Sirius find the Zoi, and some of his strategies are likely to amuse both child and adult readers.

For example, as Sirius grows into a full-size dog, Duffie requires Kathleen to leash him in the back yard during the school day. But he *must* get out, if he is to search for the Zoi. He knows how to slip his collar, and Tibbles can teach him (they are now friends) to slide the bolts on the garden gate with a clumsy paw. All but the top one, which is choked with rust. Tibbles can't lubricate it, nor Sirius. Sol can, though his method is strikingly indirect. He causes the neighbors two houses down to switch to oil heat, and then he arranges a little accident when the first delivery comes. Droplets of oil land all over the garden gate, soaking the bolt and enabling Duffie to collect substantial damages from the oil company. It is a fine comic scene.

This book does have one flaw, at least from an adult point of view. It is a flaw common to all of Diana Wynne Jones's books. Her wicked adult characters, like Duffie, are too wicked. The good ones, like Miss Smith, are so generous, sensitive, loving, and tireless as to defy all plausibility.

I'm not sure this is a flaw from a child's point of view. A wholly wicked stepmother and an entirely good fairy god-mother are probably just what children like best to read about. And if the child heroine, living with a prosperous family to whom she is closely related, gets up on Christmas morning to find she has no presents whatsoever, except one lone book taken from her uncle—well, that just makes her eventual triumph all the sweeter.

What is that triumph? I'm not going to tell you. I'm just going to say that one day Kathleen may have f-friends in v-very high p-places. She might even live off p-planet.

Dogsbody.
Diana Wynne Jones. 1975.

❧ 28 ❧

The Peaceable Kingdom

INETEEN FORTY-FOUR was one of the bloodier years in American history. On one side of the globe we invaded France; and just on D-Day alone something like ten thousand young Americans became casualties. A good many young Englishmen and Germans did, too. On the other side of the globe, American troops were busy retaking New Guinea and the Philippines—killing young Japanese soldiers, and being killed by them.

Back home, some people lived and breathed war, but others began to long for peace. They found it heartrending to see so much death, so many young men cut off at eighteen or twenty-three, so much of the world ravaged. One of those who longed for peace was an artist and writer (and World War I veteran) named Robert Lawson. And in that war year he published a fantasy about the Peaceable Kingdom—the place, you will remember, where no creature has enemies, where the lion lies down with the lamb.

There are no lambs or lions in Lawson's book, but that's only because it takes place in western Connecticut, where sheep have been scarce since the settling of Montana, where lions haven't lived in millennia. Whatever *does* live in western Connecticut figures in the book. There are rabbits, deer, woodchucks, skunks, squirrels, mice, cutworms, dogs,

cats, and human beings, among others. One family of rabbits—Father, Mother, Little Georgie, and old Uncle Analdas—provide the central characters. They are very much
storybook rabbits, closer to Brer Rabbit and Peter Rabbit
than they are to the lapinically accurate wild rabbits of *Watership Down*. They don't wear clothes, though, except that
sometimes Mother Rabbit puts an apron on when she is
making peavine and lettuce soup. A good thing, too. Lawson's fifty wonderful illustrations would be much less wonderful if they hid the animals under clothing.

As the book opens, there is already a greater degree of
amity between different species than is usual. It is especially striking between predator and prey. For example,
there is a gray fox living on the hill: the dreaded *homba* of
Watership Down. But this fox and Father Rabbit are old
friends. Again, the daring young fieldmouse named Willie,
prey par excellence, is on good terms with every animal on
the hill. This is a peaceful, even a loving community.

One reason is that all the wild animals have a common
enemy: us. Or, at any rate, the people of Connecticut, plus
their cats and dogs. The human beings shoot, poison, trap,
and gas the wild animals, and they also loose their preda-
tory pets. The first time you see Father Rabbit and Fox together, Fox is just thanking the rabbit for taking two hounds
off his trail the day before, and thus saving his life. "You
handled them very skillful, very," says Fox, "and I am
obliged to you."

At the same time, to be sure, the wild animals do wish
human beings to be around. They have gotten used to raiding our gardens, eating apples in our orchards and clover in
our fields, garbage in our cans. They count on it. The animals even have a ceremony called Dividing Night, when
they meet in solemn conclave and portion out raiding rights
to the human garden.

Lately there has been nothing to portion. For a whole
year, as the book begins, no human family has been living in

the big brick farmhouse on the hill. For two years before that, a nongardening family had lived there. They planted nothing, fertilized nothing, let even the clover die out. It has been a lean time for the animals.

But now word has spread like wildfire. New Folks coming.

The new folks do come, and the main story begins. Very simply, it is the declaration of peace between us and the wild animals. As a side benefit, and in contrast to the destruction going on in Europe (there were Normandy towns 90 percent destroyed in 1944), the house and farm are to be repaired, restored, renewed.

The winding down of hostilities starts, actually, with the cat the human couple bring with them. He is a very large tiger-striped cat named Mr. Muldoon. Uncle Analdas Rabbit, who has been both a fighter and a boaster all his life, is all set to start a war. The cat is dozing on the sunny doorstep. "I'd just as soon walk up and kick him in the face—will, too, one of these days," says Uncle Analdas.

But the cat, who is elderly, has no interest in fighting rabbits. He ignores Analdas's challenge. He doesn't even catch mice. There comes a time when Willie Fieldmouse and several of his cousins form a half-circle around the sleeping cat, "jeering and making faces. They hopped up and down and sang insultingly,

> Mr. Muldoon
> Is a raccoon,
> Phew! Phew! Phew!"

Would a self-respecting cat put up with such effrontery? Yes.

> Mr. Muldoon just put a paw over his ear and continued to slumber.
> "Shucks," grunted Uncle Analdas, "he couldn't danger *nobody*."

The cat is merely indifferent—until late in the book, when he befriends Georgie. But the human couple are actively friendly. They plant a garden twice the size they think they'll need, and, to the amazement of the locals, do not fence it. They *expect* it to be raided, and want there to be plenty for everybody. When one of their visitors nearly runs over a rabbit on their long driveway, they put up a sign. "Please Drive Carefully On Account of Small Animals," it reads.

And in the great climax scene of the book, they erect a statue of St. Francis of Assisi, with a magnificent feeding station for birds and animals around it. Salt for the deer, buckwheat (from their own field) for the woodchuck, something for everybody. In gratitude, the animals hardly touch the unfenced garden; in fact, they patrol and protect it. Mole and his three brothers keep the cutworms out entirely. The locals, who fence and shoot and poison, and whose gardens are raided constantly, can hardly believe it.

Rabbit Hill could easily have been a sentimental book. Several things save it. One is the plentiful comedy, which centers on Uncle Analdas and on a gluttonous skunk with a passion for what he always calls "garbidge." Another is the exact opposite: an occasional hint, not of tragedy, but of real-world pain, a glimpse of the Nature that seeks no peace but stays forever red in tooth and claw.

For example, though in his old age Mr. Muldoon tolerates and even comes to like rabbits, Lawson never pretends that cats as a species are getting peaceable. There's an early scene where Father and Mother Rabbit, trying to make Georgie careful, remind him how many of their relatives have been lost to cats: "I hope the lesson to be learned from the untimely feline ends of our grandchildren Minnie and Arthur, Wilfred, Sarah, Constance, Sarepta, Hogarth, and Clarence will not be lightly passed over by you," Father says, looking hard at Georgie.

Of course there is an element of comedy both in Father's

grandiloquent style (he is from Kentucky, and always talks like this), and in the sheer quantity of lost grandchildren, rabbits being so notoriously fecund. But Lawson takes care that the incident not turn wholly comic. He illustrates a scene that appears nowhere in the text—couldn't, since it depicts a psychological state, not an event. A sorrowful Mother Rabbit is shown looking at a row of beautifully drawn tombstones. Each is inscribed with the name of a dead grandchild. It might almost be a military cemetery in France.

But the main preventive is Lawson's artistic skill, his gift for drawing animals. (None of the human beings in the book ever appears in an illustration.) Maybe twice Lawson makes an animal cute. But mostly he is too full of truth for that. His rabbits are far closer to Albrecht Dürer's than they are to Warner Brothers.

I grant, *Rabbit Hill* is a light book. It is, at least, compared to the epic grandeur of something like *Watership Down*. The Peaceable Kingdom itself is a lighthearted place, especially when compared to the battlefield we all live on. That's what makes it such a joy to visit.

Rabbit Hill.
Robert Lawson. 1944.

◆§ *29* ◈◆

If They Will Sign the Treaty, He May Kiss Me

FOUR SHIPS ARE approaching a foreign coast. They are not expected and not welcome. Especially since two of them appear to be breathing fire.

More Europeans to bother the King of the Jolliginki? No, this is Commodore Perry of the U.S. Navy, coming to bother the Japanese. President Millard Fillmore has sent him to open Japan, which has been closed to foreign visitors since the year 1636. It is now 1853.

Hundreds of American whaling ships, like Melville's *Pequod,* are cruising the Pacific, and with some frequency one or another of them gets caught in a typhoon and wrecked on the coast of Japan. Surviving crew members wind up in Japanese jails. The first aim of Perry's mission is to put a stop to that. Second: Promote trade. Third: Get in ahead of the British, French, and Russians, all of whom are itching to open closed doors.

There are plenty of books about Perry in Japan, including Perry's own *Narrative of the Expedition,* various journals kept by his officers and men, and many accounts by twentieth-century historians. But Rhoda Blumberg has done something special, and has produced a really fine book for older children. For those whose taste runs to the exotic, an irresistible book. And it's all true.

Two things distinguish Ms. Blumberg's book from the many others. One is that she knows and tells both sides: how the Japanese looked to the Americans, but also how the Americans looked to the Japanese. This she does both in her text and in the illustrations, of which there are about sixty.

In the text, for example, you get to sample the reports made to the shogun's government by a man named Manjiro, who knows more about Americans than anyone else in Japan. Reason: His fishing boat was wrecked in a typhoon when he was fourteen, and he was rescued by a homeward bound American whaler. He lived for ten years in Fairhaven, Massachusetts, and then in California, before he slipped back into Japan.

Manjiro has all sorts of things to tell the government, many of them not in the least related to Perry's ships or mission. For example, in America, Manjiro reports, "It is customary to read books in the toilet." It is also customary to have a dinky little wedding, followed by that extraordinary thing, a honeymoon: "For their wedding ceremony, the Americans merely make a proclamation to the gods, and become married, after which they usually go on a sightseeing trip to the mountains. They are lewd by nature, but otherwise well-behaved."

The illustrations are more interesting yet. About a third of them are done by Americans, mostly by the two official artists who accompanied the expedition. Some are just stunning, like a painting of the augmented squadron that Perry brought for his second visit in 1854. Nine warships under full sail, a sight of heartrending beauty.

But it's the two-thirds by Japanese artists that give one to think. Many are sketches of Americans: of Perry himself, of Captain Joel Abbott of the U.S.S. *Macedonian,* of common sailors on shore leave. Without exception, we have long sharp noses and too much hair. We look fierce, barbaric. One reason this book is for big children and not small ones is that the Japanese portrait of Commodore Perry on page 23 could easily give a person nightmares. What might give a person a fit of laughter, on the other hand, is the illustrated chart that instructs Japanese men how to dress like Westerners. The Japanese artist didn't intend it as a joke; he is quite serious with his cravats and top hats and heraldically crossed black umbrellas. But to think that our ancestors deliberately chose to dress like that, and that the silly nineteenth-century Japanese wanted to copy them, how could it fail to tickle a jeans-clad twelve year old?

Ms. Blumberg's second great strength is the richness of context she provides. It's remarkable. I have read a fair amount of Japanese history, and have spent time in Japan besides. I thought I knew most things about Perry's expedition and its context. I was wrong. To take just one example, the traffic across the Pacific in that remote era was far greater than I had realized. Consider the spring of 1854. While Perry and the nine ships he had brought for the second visit were still anchored in the northern port of Hakodate, what should come sailing in but one of those American whalers? The *Eliza Mason,* twenty-one months out of New Bedford. No fear of jail now, with the great guns of the *Powhatan* and the *Macedonian* trained on the port.

The whaling captain and his wife and young son are on shore in a flash. The wife, Abigail Jernegan, is the first Western woman to set foot in Japan in about 240 years. She happily spends the night on shore, and when she goes back to the *Eliza Mason* the next day, she is soon followed by a messenger carrying a beautifully wrapped package. Inside is something she forgot on shore: an ordinary pin.

Fifteen days after the squadron left, the first tourist ship arrived. It was actually a private yacht, the *Lady Pierce,* owned by a Connecticut millionaire named Silas Burrows. He had no idea that the Japanese had just signed the Treaty

of Kanagawa, thus reopening the country to visitors. He
had made his own arrangements for slipping through the
closed door: He had brought another Japanese castaway
along to be his excuse for stopping. A man of imagination,
he had also had some special gold coins minted in San
Francisco, to give as presents. He gave them out, all right,
but very soon he got them back. Like official American
coinage then and now, his special coins had the word "Liberty" stamped on them. Liberty was not a thing the shogun-
al government altogether approved of. The coins were collected from the recipients and returned to Mr. Burrows.

American children are said to be notoriously weak in history and geography. Books like this seem to me to be an
ideal strengthener. There is no dumbing down. There is just
such richness of detail that the child is apt to forget all
about TV, and go right on reading.

Oh, one last thing. Who said that about getting kissed if
they'd only sign the treaty? That was Commodore Perry, age
fifty-nine. He has just been entertaining five Japanese commissioners and their retinues aboard the *Powhatan*. He has
served a great deal of liquor. One of the commissioners is a
bit drunk. As he leaves, "He hugged the Commodore so
hard that Perry's new epaulettes were crushed. Perry did
not mind the hug. 'Oh,' he said to his officers, 'if they will
only sign the Treaty, he may kiss me.'"

Didn't know dignified commodores could joke like that,
did you?

Commodore Perry in the Land of the Shogun.
Rhoda Blumberg. 1985.

❦ *30* ❦

A Book That Works Like a
Charm

"THE ISLAND OF GONT, a single mountain that lifts its peak a mile above the storm-wracked Northeast Sea, is a land famous for wizards." So begins one of the three or four best sword-and-sorcery novels written in this century. I mean Ursula K. Le Guin's *A Wizard of Earthsea.*

A qualification is needed immediately. It's not exactly a *sword*-and-sorcery novel; lesser books are that. It's a staff-and-sorcery novel. The only characters who use swords are some yellow-haired Kargish barbarians who invade Gont when Ged, the hero of the book, is a boy of twelve. They and their bronze swords figure only in the first chapter. (They are all dead at the end of the chapter.) The wooden staff carried by a true wizard plays the power role in this book.

One other qualification: Though there are sorcerers in the book, there are not many. Most of the people in Earthsea who can say charms or lay spells or do the kind of chanting that produces enchantment are wizards. The distinction is an important one. Look up sorcery in a good dictionary, and you will find that sorcerers get their power by being able to control evil spirits. Sorcery, like witchcraft, is black magic.

If you now look up wizard, you will see that it is merely the word "wise" with the suffix -ard. That suffix indicates something habitual. A drunkard is in the habit of drinking too much, a sluggard lies around a lot, and a wizard is habitually wise. One way to describe *A Wizard of Earthsea* is as the story of how Ged acquired wisdom.

There are other ways to describe it, of course. For example, it is a superb adventure story, cast in the form of a quest. It is also a profound look at the uses and dangers of power. It is a triumph of style. And best of all, it is the calling into being of an entire world.

Any novel creates a world, to be sure—that's the sole and adequate justification for the phrase "creative writing," which would otherwise be unbearably pretentious. Works of heroic fantasy such as *Earthsea* tend to create especially elaborate worlds. Their authors invent languages, design new continents or construct whole new planets, plant strange trees. But Le Guin has done what it is given to very few to do. She has made a new world seem inevitable.

Any competent novelist can make up some words, set some rules, invent a place, and draw a map of it for a frontispiece—and it all seems quite arbitrary. You feel the words could be changed to other words—the creatures called inyahs could be called faalgorns—and nothing lost. Not here. In the case of Earthsea, you would think Le Guin had discovered this world, not made it up. I mean that as the very highest praise.

Ged, the central character, is the son of the bronzesmith in the village of Ten Alders. His mother is dead, but his somewhat scary aunt is very much alive; she is the village witch. Ged gets his first lessons from her when he is seven years old. Five years later, when the Kargs pull up their longships on the beaches of Gont, he knows a good many of the minor spells, including one for what is called fogweaving. The mist he is able to hold over the village when the sun should have burned it off is what enables the

mere eighteen men of Ten Alders to ambush the detach-
ment of Kargs who come up their valley intent on rape and
destruction. Such spells normally work only briefly, and
Ged by holding the mist almost an hour greatly overspends
his strength. He lies in a coma for five days.

The news that a boy of twelve could bind such a spell
soon spreads across Gont. It leads first to his being taken on
as an apprentice by Ogion the silent, the greatest wizard on
Gont, and about a year later to his sailing to Roke, the island of wizards. On Roke there is a school for boys like
Ged—those who can, in the old and true sense of the word,
charm. Of, if you prefer, those who have the ability to fasci-
nate. (Look *that* word up sometime.)

In school the hundred or so students learn first the com-
paratively easy arts of illusion, and later the difficult and
dangerous arts of summoning and changing. Ged is perhaps
the most gifted boy of the whole hundred; unfortunately, he
is also one of the most easily put on his mettle. As a child
on Gont, Ged had herded goats as well as working the bel-
lows at his father's forge and occasionally learning a spell
from his aunt. He feels vulnerable to gibes about goat-boys.

Stung by the subtle and well-bred mockery of a fellow
student whose father is a prince on the great island of
Havnor, Ged shows off his power by raising a spirit from the
dead. In so doing he accidentally opens a channel that
should have stayed shut. He is very nearly killed by the
creature that comes through it, and that stays in the world,
and that he must face again and again, and eventually challenge. By then he has left the school at Roke, has his staff
as wizard, and is a very powerful magician.

Ways of approaching magic range from the ludicrous
through the lighthearted and on to the grand and serious.
Puff the Magic Dragon is ludicrous. Jane's metal charm in
Half Magic that grants only half of what you ask is lighthearted. The magic in E. Nesbit is a bit more serious, and
the magic in *The Children of Green Knowe* is sad, solemn,

and strong. But the magic in *A Wizard of Earthsea* goes deeper than any of these. It has more in common with the supernatural elements in *Beowulf* than it does with any let's-pretend twentieth-century book. (Tolkien, in case you're wondering, I do not consider let's-pretend.)

Even in actual language, *A Wizard of Earthsea* and its three sequels are kin to the sagas and to Old English. The extreme case, perhaps, is Le Guin's description of the tower on Roke where the Master Namer lives. He is one of the ten mages who run the school and who also direct much of the magic of the world. Here is her introduction of the tower: "Grim it stood above the northern cliffs, grey were the clouds over the seas of winter, endless the lists and ranks of names that the Namer's eight pupils must learn."

The three-part parallel structure and the use of first-word alliteration instead of last-word rhyme are the very signatures of heroic fantasy back in the age of belief, when it didn't seem to be fantasy at all. This sentence I believe to be Le Guin's quiet bow to that age. The book itself is not written in any such stylized way—it wouldn't be so intensely readable to people at the end of the twentieth century if it were. But it *is* grand and serious. And Le Guin is very clear that if you fail to take either yourself or the world seriously, you do so only at the risk of your soul. Our culture mostly teaches otherwise, and this book makes a fine antidote. It will hold an imaginative child spellbound.

A Wizard of Earthsea.
Ursula K. Le Guin. 1968.

Honorable Mention

*E*VERY CHILD WHO READS a lot has the capacity for almost infinite repetition. Adults think they also have this capacity just because they reread the works of Jane Austen every five or ten years, or go back one more time to Willa Cather. But what I'm talking about is the child who first reads, let us say, *The White Company* at the age of nine, reads it again at ten, at eleven—and only stops about the time he or she is getting assigned *Julius Caesar* in high school.

There were dozens of such books in my early life. Some, like Jeffery Farnol's *The Amateur Gentleman,* I knew were high-class junk even as I first read them. So it was a guilty pleasure to go back and back as I stumbled into my teens. Others I would have said were great literature, if I had had the concept of great literature then, which I didn't. A few really were great if quirky great literature, like Mark Twain's *Life on the Mississippi.* But most of the books I loved came in between. There are several that I now see to have enormous faults, but which I loved back then and which I still respect. There are three in particular, that though I won't give them the honor of an essay, I still can't bear not to mention.

One is precisely *The White Company.* This is Sir Arthur Conan Doyle wearing—not his other hat, but his helmet and shining armor. Everybody knows Sherlock Holmes and Baker Street at the end of the nineteenth century. Many fewer know Sir Nigel Loring in the middle of the fourteenth.

The White Company itself is historical fact. In the year 1360, England and France signed a peace treaty. A group of English men-at-arms, led by Sir John Hawkwood, wished to go on fighting—they didn't particularly care who. So they rode down to Italy, where they became immensely success-ful free-lance soldiers. They became known throughout Tuscany as the White Company.

Doyle imagines that only half the company went to Italy, the other half preferring to stay in northern Europe and do their free-lancing, pillaging, jousting, drinking, and wench-ing there. Sir Nigel Loring, who is not historical and whom Doyle is thus free to make the epitome of chivalry, com-mands the northern Company.

The book is about as romantic as a story about knight-hood could possibly be. It is also full of one-dimensional characters (some of them pretty vivid all the same), echoes of Sir Walter Scott, plot coincidences, privileging of nine-teenth-century Protestant virtues, and so on. I cannot rec-ommend it wholeheartedly. But with half my heart I ea-gerly do.

Clare Mallison's *The Wooster-Poosters* is for a much younger audience. The Wooster-Poosters (unfortunate name) are a family composed entirely of dogs—Aberdeen terriers, to be exact, commonly known as Scotties. They don't live in Scot-land, though, but in a nameless American town. The year is 1931. There's Annie Laurie, who seems to be a single mother, way back then. There's Angus, most probably her son, who is not yet old enough to read. (These dogs learn to read and write at the appropriate age; they wear clothes, in which they look ridiculous, walk on their hind legs, and matter-of-factly function in the human world.) Finally, there's Cousin Dusty, a fun-loving and rather selfish older boy-dog.

In a small and local way, this book is an American equiv-
alent of Doctor Dolittle. That is, it's an absurdist comedy.
The book describes a trip—not by ship to Africa, but by
local bus to an amusement park. At the climax Angus,
rather ineptly disguised as a human baby, is competing for a
$500 prize, a vast sum in that Depression year. What's so
funny is the contrast between how seriously the Scotties
take everything and how ridiculous they look. It might even
be funnier now than it was in 1931.

So why not an out-and-out recommendation? Well, first
because it's a hard book to find, and why frustrate you? But
mostly because, though the pictures are inspired, the writing isn't. There are four or five wonderful lines, but the rest
is just serviceable. What of Clare Mallison herself? I can
learn nothing of the person who wrote the adequate text
and drew those marvelous pictures except that this seems
to be her only book. Pity.

That small output puts her in maximum contrast with
the last writer I shall bring up. George MacDonald, born in
Scotland in 1824, was as prolific as Noel Streatfeild and E.
Nesbit. He published thirty adult novels. An ordained minister (he startled his nineteenth-century Scottish congrega-
tion by his freely voiced belief that animals as well as
human beings could find Christian salvation—and if he is
right, I think Annie Laurie has a bright future). I'll start
over. An ordained minister, he published several volumes of
his sermons. Somewhat more volumes of poetry.

But his best work is his fantasy writing for children, and
I think the best of *that* is the story "The Light Princess."
She is an enchanting young woman, light in two senses.
She is not subject to gravity, and she is not serious. Her
conversion to gravity—by a prince, of course—makes a
wonderful story.

MacDonald also wrote three full-length fantasy novels
for children. Two of them, *The Princess and the Goblin* and
The Princess and Curdie, still have power. The third one, *At*

the Back of the North Wind, I think is quite skippable. Too preachy, with the author in the pulpit.

A carping critic might say that all of MacDonald is too preachy, and there is some truth to the charge. That's why "The Light Princess" is grounded back here, instead of floating triumphantly through an essay of her own. And yet, and yet, I can't help hoping that some son or daughter or niece or nephew or godchild or small friend of yours gets to meet her and her prince.

The White Company.
Sir Arthur Conan Doyle. 1891.

The Wooster-Poosters.
Clare Mallison. 1931.

The Light Princess and Other Fairy Stories.
George MacDonald. 1890.
(The book first appeared in 1867 as
Dealings with the Fairies.)

Epilogue

SUPPOSE YOU WANT to get hold of one of these books. I want to help. Here's a list of them, alphabetized by author, giving prices and editions. After some indecision, I included the three honorable mentions. Sixteen of these books are available on cassette, and after even longer indecision, I included information about them.

What held me back? I'm not entirely sure that audio tapes for children's books should exist. Children are not driving to work and listening to tapes in the car. Children, at least young ones, mainly encounter books in their own bedrooms, at bedtime. Would they really rather listen to a tape than snuggle with a parent who is reading aloud? Would the parent really rather turn bedtime over to a voice from a machine?

Still, the voices are there, and most of them belong to highly skilled performers. I didn't exclude them.

What I *did* exclude, with no hesitation at all, is abridgments. To the best of my knowledge, every book or cassette listed here is complete, unabridged, honestly given as the author wrote it.

One last comment. Publishers tend to let books go in and out of print with great rapidity, and they are sometimes known to raise prices. Very soon after I complete the list it will begin to be inaccurate. But I think it will stay reasonably useful for some years.

As for the ten books that are out of print just now, most can be found quite easily in second-hand bookstores, and nearly all will be on the shelves of any good library.

BIBLIOGRAPHY

Richard Adams, *Watership Down*. Avon $5.99. Books on Tape, $88 (can be rented for $18.50). Literate Ear, $68.20 (rental, $10.80).

Rhoda Blumberg, *Commodore Perry in the Land of the Shogun*. Lothrop, hardcover, $16.

Lucy Boston, *The Children of Green Knowe*. Harcourt Brace, $6.95. Audio Books, $24.95.

Lord Brabourne, *Tales at Tea-Time*. Out of print.

Leslie Brooke, *Johnny Crow's Garden*. Out of print.

Robert Burch, *Queenie Peavey*. Puffin, $3.99. Live Oak, a one-tape dramatization of the book plus a paperback copy of it, $14.95.

Lolah Burford, *The Vision of Stephen*. Out of print.

Joanna Cole and Bruce Degen, *The Magic School Bus, Lost in the Solar System*. Scholastic, $4.99.

George Dasent, *East o' the Sun and West o' the Moon*. Out of print. (Several books with this title are in print, but they bear no relation to Dasent.)

Arthur Conan Doyle, *The White Company*. Morrow Junior Books, hardcover, $20. Buccaneer, hardcover, $24.95.

Edward Eager, *Half Magic*. Harcourt Brace, $6.

Wanda Gág, *Millions of Cats*. Paper Star $4.95. Coward-McCann, hardcover, $12.95.

Rumer Godden, *The Dolls' House*. Puffin, $4.99. Peter Smith, hardcover, $18. Listening Library, one cassette plus a copy of the paperback, $15.98.

Virginia Hamilton, *The Planet of Junior Brown*. Collier Books, $3.95. Recorded Books, $34 (rental, $11.50).

Nathaniel Hawthorne, *Tanglewood Tales* and *A Wonder-Book for Boys and Girls*. Airmont, $2.50. Buccaneer, hardcover, $22.95. Library of America, hardcover, $37.50; paperback, $13.95. Books on Tape, $30 (rental, $9.95).

Laurence Housman, *The Rat-Catcher's Daughter*. Out of print.

———. *The Golden Sovereign*. Out of print.

Diana Wynne Jones, *Dogsbody*. Out of print.

Robert Lawson, *Rabbit Hill*. Puffin, $3.99. Viking, hardcover, $15.99. Recorded Books, $18 (rental, $8.50).

Ursula K. Le Guin, *A Wizard of Earthsea*. Bantam, $6.50. Atheneum, hardcover, $16.95. Recorded Books, $40 (rental, $13.50).

Anne Lindbergh, *Nick of Time*. Little Brown, hardcover, $15.95.

Hugh Lofting, *The Story of Doctor Dolittle*. In Buccaneer, *Doctor Dolittle: A Treasury*, $25.95. Books on Tape, $18 (rental $8.50). Blackstone Audio, $17.95.

George MacDonald, *The Light Princess*. Eerdmans, $7. Farrar Straus, hardcover $15; paper $4.95. Listening Library, paperback and cassette, $15.98.

Clare Mallison, *The Wooster-Poosters*. Out of print.

Jean Merrill, *The Pushcart War*. Dell, $3.99. HarperCollins, hardcover, $14.89. Recorded Books, $34 (rental, $11.50).

E. Nesbit, *The Railway Children*. Puffin, $3.99. Brimax, $5.98. Chivers North America, cassette, $32.95. Audio Book Contractors, $29.95 (rental, $10.95).

Mary Norton, *The Borrowers*. Harcourt Brace, $6 paper and $15 hardcover. Chivers North America, cassette, $18.95.

Robert O'Brien, *Z for Zachariah*. Collier Books, $5.25.

Ernest Thompson Seton, *Two Little Savages*. Dover, $7.95. Amereon, hardcover, $21.95.

Margery Sharp, *The Rescuers*. Little Brown, $4.95. Recorded Books, $26 (rental, $9.50).

Dodie Smith, *I Capture the Castle*. Out of print as a book. Chivers North America, ten cassette tapes, $84.95.

Zilpha Keatley Snyder, *The Egypt Game*. Dell, $4.50. Recorded Books, $34 (rental, $11.50).

Mary Stolz, *A Dog on Barkham Street*. Trophy, $4.50.

Noel Streatfeild, *Movie Shoes*. Out of print.

P. L. Travers, *I Go by Sea, I Go by Land*. Out of print.

Sylvia Townsend Warner, *The Kingdoms of Elfin*. Out of print.

T. H. White, *Mistress Masham's Repose*. Out of print.

LIBRARY OF CONGRESS CATALOGING-IN-PUBLICATION DATA
Perrin, Noel.
A child's delight / Noel Perrin.
    p.   cm.
Collection of essays originally appearing as columns in the
Washington post and the Los Angeles times.
Published for Dartmouth College.
Includes bibliographical references (p.   ).
ISBN 0–87451–840–7 (cl. : alk. paper) : ISBN 1–58465–352–3 (pa. : alk. paper)
1. Children's stories, English—History and criticism.
2. Children's stories, American—History and criticism.
3. Children's stories, English—Book reviews.   4. Young adult
fiction, English—Book reviews.   5. Children's stories, American—
Book reviews.   6. Young adult fiction, American—Book reviews.
7. Children—Books and reading.   8. Canon (Literature)   I. Title.
PR830.C513P47   1997
823.009'9282—dc21   97–28220